This edition of

michael marshall smith
an annotated bibliography

is limited to
200 signed hardcovers
and 300 unsigned paperbacks

This is # 21

michael marshall smith
an annotated bibliography

compiled by lavie tidhar
annotations by michael marshall smith

PS Publishing, 2004

FIRST EDITION

Introduction © Copyright 2004 Lavie Tidhar

Bibliography © Copyright 2004 Lavie Tidhar

Annotations © Copyright 2004 Michael Marshall Smith

Interior design © Copyright 2004 Mark Roberts

Alarm Clock illustration © Copyright Zaz Kee 1998

———————————

Published in 2004 by PS Publishing LLP

Hardcover: 1-904619-05-3
Paperback: 1-904619-04-5

PS Publishing LLP
Hamilton House
4 Park Avenue
Harrogate
HG2 9BQ
ENGLAND

http://www.pspublishing.co.uk

email: crowth1@attglobal.net

———————————

Michael Marshall Smith: http://www.michaelmarshallsmith.com

———————————

Lavie Tidhar: http://www.users.globalnet.co.uk/~lavie

———————————

Mark Roberts: http://www.chimeric.co.uk

ACKNOWLEDGEMENTS

With thanks to the following people:

Dirk Berger
John Berlyne
Jay Caselberg
Suzanne Chalke
Stacy Cowley
Peter Crowther
Melanie Dymond Harper
Tim Herklots
Howard Hymanson
Stephen Jones
Archie Maskill
Paul Miller
Alain Nevant
Jim Rickards
Al Sarrantonio
Bill Schafer
Peter Schneider
Jim Seels
Chris Smith

CONTENTS

Introduction - **10**

Notes on the Bibliographic System - **12**

Novels, Novellas and Collections - **14**

Limited Editions - selected covers - ***32***

First Editions - selected covers - ***33***

Short Stories - **34**

Non-English Editions - selected covers - ***72***

Selected Non-Fiction - **74**

Selected Book Design - **76**

Selected Studies - **77**

michael marshall smith
an annotated bibliography

INTRODUCTION

Michael Marshall Smith appeared on the literary scene in 1990, with the short story **The Man Who Drew Cats**, which went on to win the coveted British Fantasy Award. Since then, he has established himself, in a very short time, as one of the most important and original new voices in the current British genre revival. Over the course of a decade, quotes such as "a name to watch" and "one of the up and coming giants of the field" have been replaced with "storytelling skill that can only be described as pure genius", "tour de force", "stunning" and "breathtaking". "Start collecting his work now!" advises a British Fantasy Society newsletter - an advice which I have unwittingly followed and which has led, over time, to the compilation of the volume you are now holding.

In attempting such a bibliography, it should be questioned why Smith has attracted such a loyal readership; why two of his novels have been optioned for film by leading Hollywood producers; and indeed, what it is in his writing that appeals to people from as far afield as Japan and Israel.

Smith, I believe, is more than a writer of exciting stories (though exciting and suspenseful they are). Rather, he is the voice of a generation, embodying in his writing the conflicts and preoccupations of our age.

We live in a post-modern world: on the fracture between Fordist, Keynsian modes of production and government - and the free-market, capitalist chaos of a new, globalised planet. Our society is obsessed with consumption; our world is filled with the symbols of wealth, the fads of a people more concerned with image than product. Yet behind the façade of this service society, underneath the floor of the so-called information age, the planet is teeming with new inequality, with injustice and repression and war.

Smith is a writer who goes underneath this façade; who knows our obsessions and fears and dreams and who comments on this new world reality with a mastery that is wholly literary, and entirely of today. In **Only Forward**, for example, we are exposed to both a fragmented city, a future London split along the lines of special-interest groups, of vying political ideas and ideologies; and to the dream world of Jeamland, where the signs and symbols of our generation are penetrated by his "poor man's Philip Marlowe." Indeed, as Matthew Hills argues in a recent article, "each of Smith's detective protagonists, to varying degrees, acts as the 'social detective,'" and in his fantasies, "consumption itself becomes increasingly all-consuming." Thus, in **Spares** it is human beings who become commodities, while dreams and memories can be paid off in **One of Us**. Smith's detectives struggle to make sense of a world at once familiar and alien: malls expand, a la **Alice in**

Wonderland, to immense size, becoming complete, enclosed societies. Electronic appliances, alarm-clocks and refrigerators, take on personalities, aping today's notion that buying a product is, in fact, the purchase of a certain life-style.

In his approach, Smith is more often than not a post-modernist: his novels incorporate elements of science fiction, fantasy, horror, the crime or detective novel, noir - and whichever other style or genre he finds useful. In a world where nothing is definite and boxed anymore, Smith explores the alternate styles and modes that have gone before. In that, he is similar to both the cyberpunks, that street-wise, hi-tech anarchic movement of the 1980s, and to the playful, ironic, self-referential steampunks - but Smith is not, in a post-modern sense, nostalgic, nor is he fascinated with technology for technology's sake, in as much as he is with the way society and technology affect each other.

I discovered **Spares** on a second-hand shelf in a London bookshop, and had to stay up late into the night in order to finish the book in one go. Since then, I have seen Smith's work sold in places as diverse and unlikely as Mongolia and Borneo, Singapore and Israel. His work has been translated into over fourteen languages, his short stories appear regularly in "Best Of" anthologies, and have been nominees and winners of nearly every major award in the field.

For collectors, Smith is both easy to collect and something of a challenge. Easy - because so far only four novels, and four short story collections, have been published - yet there are some editions, such as the **Only Forward** proof, or the small paperback of **When God Lived in Kentish Town**, that are now nearly impossible to find.

Finally, this bibliography goes beyond the painstaking collection of bare data; for in this volume Smith, for the first time, offers us a glimpse into the origin of his work. In his inimitable style, at times wry, at times funny, at times very serious indeed, Smith discusses his novels and short stories, offering us a window into the mind of the author who, in his turn, offers us a window into our own lives, our own world.

Here, then, is his work, in all its myriad editions, states and appearances, and here, also, are his thoughts, his comments, short breaths of stories about stories.

     Lavie Tidhar
     London
     2004

THE BIBLIOGRAPHICAL SYSTEM

There are as many ways, it seems, to compile a bibliography as there are positive numbers. A short explanation of the system used is therefore in order. Each item on the list is assigned a unique identifier, the generic format of which is capital letter/ number/lowercase letter, where capital letter stands for category, number identifies the title, and lowercase letter represents the edition. Thus, A1a is A (a book) 1 (**Only Forward**) a (first publication). This format will be followed by a dot (.) and a number if more than one state of the book exists. For example, A2v.1 is the trade state of **Spares**: The Special Edition. Once an item goes beyond 26 separate editions, a new cycle of entries starts, designated by a * symbol. Thus A2*a is the Japanese edition of **Spares**.

Proof copies are not listed as a separate edition, but rather appear after the book with the letter doubled. For example, A2aa is the proof copy of the first edition of **Spares**, which is listed as A2a. Every attempt has been made to verify if proof copies were produced for each edition, yet it should be assumed it is possible proofs were produced of which we are unaware. By listing proofs after the book publication, it becomes possible to add them to the bibliography at a later date without affecting the numbering system.

Promotional material and unique items have the same designation. Where there is a proof as well, such items will be assigned a triple letter. Promotional material tend to be comprised of book extracts, promotional postcards (collectible in themselves) and other ephemera. Unique items are one-off productions, in this instance mainly consisting of publishers' presentation copies to the author.

Publisher copies (usually designated as PC) of limited editions are not listed. These are additional copies of a limited state which are out of series, often produced for marketing and review purposes. Information on these copies is not generally available, but anything from five to one hundred copies of any given state should be assumed.

The generic format of individual entries is Identifier - Country: Publisher, Date - Format, Price, ISBN. Editors, translators and illustrators are given when known. In cases where this information has been omitted, it can be assumed to be have been unavailable.

A note on online publications:

The bibliography is composed solely of printed material. Online appearances are omitted. These include the short story **Dead Stringer for Love**, co-authored with Paul J. McAuley and Jeff VanderMeer and which appeared on the Event Horizon web site (no print edition currently exists), and **A Convenient Arrangement** which was reprinted on Dusksite.com.

Sources used:
I have used extensively a number of online sources. Most notable is Archie Maskill's superb bibliography[1] on which I have relied the most. Other important sources have been the Internet Speculative Fiction Database[2], The Locus Index to Science Fiction[3], Stephen Jones' online bibliography[4], and for **The View**, Peter Crowther's homepage, which is sadly no longer available. Michael Marshall Smith's own records have helped to substantiate, and add to, much of the material. Jim Rickards very kindly assisted with numbers for the UK print runs, while Al Sarrantonio was kind enough to provide a complete bibliography of the various editions of his 999 anthology. I have also relied to a large degree on my own collection, as well as on those of Melanie Dymond Harper and Paul Miller. The various sites of giant booksellers Amazon[5] have also proved very useful, as have the ever-changing records available from the online book-finding service, The Advanced Book Exchange[6].

1- http://www-jcr.lmh.ox.ac.uk/~spacehog/mms/
2- http://www.sfsite.com/isfdb/
3- http://www.locusmag.com/index/
4- http://www.herebedragons.co.uk/jones/
5- http://www.amazon.co.uk, http://www.amazon.com
6- http://www.abebooks.com

Notes on Robinson/Magpie/Parragon/The Book Company editions:
For Smith bibliophiles there is some confusion about a number of titles issued by the above imprints. These were mostly anthologies edited by Stephen Jones containing a Smith story (**The Giant Book of Frankenstein**, for example). Jones offers the following explanation for these multiple imprints:

"During the 1990s Robinson went into partnership with UK book distributor Parragon to reissue some of its titles in cheap editions. Most of the titles were reissued by Robinson under three imprints: Magpie (a Robinson imprint distributed in the UK - at varying prices - and throughout the commonwealth, for example India); Parragon (for 'instant remainder' outlets in the UK - places like Woolworths, usually for around £2.99); and The Book Company, for distribution in Australia. Distribution was erratic, but the dates listed reflect first printing. Some titles were still in circulation a few years later, while others were actually reprinted. Almost all the titles were printed in the UK simultaneously and then shipped. The only actual difference is in the imprints and copyright pages."

A Novels, Novellas and Collections

A1 ONLY FORWARD

"**Only Forward** is probably the most fun I've ever had writing. Only **The Vaccinator** (and maybe a few of the short stories) have come close to it, in the lowness of the grief involved per unit written word.

"Partly I think this was because I'd never written a novel before, and so didn't realise there was anything to be afraid of. I'd decided it was about time I tried a novel, and so I did. Nobody was expecting it: there was no deadline, no expectation or fear that it might - or might not - be like or unlike something that I had done before. I set myself no rules whatsoever, deciding not to concern myself with fitting any particular genre or expectation. All of my previous prose had been set in the present day, and fell more-or-less into the arena of contemporary 'horror' - tales of unease and the unusual. As soon as I started writing **Only Forward** it became obvious that it was set in some kind of future: it was also clear that I wanted to put humour in it - something I hadn't really done for years, since my comedy-writing days for the BBC. Both of these elements took it so far away from my previous work that I decided to just go with the initial ideas and see where they took me.

"The initial ideas boiled down to a voice; a couple of notions I'd mainly culled from own dreams; and a few suspicions about what the underlying story might be about.

"I wrote the novel in my spare time and at weekends, often nudged along the way by minor events in my 'real' life. I was wandering around central London in a lunch hour, for example, when I happened to notice a small store called Jeamland. It immediately struck me that this might be how a young child might pronounce 'Dream Land' - and another part of the emerging back story fell into place, as it coalesced both consciously and unconsciously in my mind. Other parts, like the segmented city and the digitised jungle, came from my own dream land, and were woven in largely because they just felt right. The story evolved and took me with it, often feeling more as if I was midwifing it rather than being responsible for its creation. It's often observed that the novel could be seen as falling into two halves: one more light-hearted and apparently trivial; the second darker and more serious. This is true, and something I was aware of at the time. Many of the short stories also follow this pattern. In this way the novel remains consistent with the more horror-based pattern I had established in the shorter fiction: setting up a world (both external and psychological) and then allowing the truer threads of darkness to become more visible.

"**Only Forward** took me just under six months to write. When I finished it, I sent it straight to an agent who had recently contacted me, offering representation. She packed it straight off to Jane Johnson at HarperCollins in the UK, who agreed - in fairly short order - to publish the novel.

"I make no apologies for the ludicrous ease of the whole affair. I've paid for it since, not least in the shape of the people who keep telling me it's still my best book..."

A1a - United Kingdom: HarperCollins 1994 - a paperback original, ISBN: 0586217746. Four verified print runs comprising approximately 35,000 copies sold and 10,000 remaindered. The first printing was released in two variants, priced at £5.99 and £4.99 respectively. All subsequent printings were priced at £4.99*. The fourth printing omits the Tory Amos quote due to copyright reasons.

    A1aa - Proof copy in black printed wraps. Priced at £0.00 on rear cover. About 25% thicker than **A1a**. 250 copies are believed to have been printed, with only 50-100 estimated to still exist.

A1b - as "Enkele Reis" - Holland: Luitingh 1994 - trade paperback, unpriced, ISBN: 9024512182. Translated by Victor van der Steen.

A1c - as "Stark, Der Traumdetektiv" - Germany: Bastei Lübbe Taschenbücher 1994 - paperback priced at 12.90DM, ISBN 3404241940. Translated by Bernhard Kempen.

A1d - as "Choris Epistrophe" - Greece: Medusa 1995 - paperback, unpriced, ISBN: 9607014197.

A1e - as "Enkele Reis" - Holland: Poema-Pocket (Luitingh) 1997 - paperback, ISBN 9024510686. Translated by Victor van der Steen.

---

* While HarperCollins were unable to confirm the reason for the two variants, it seems most likely the initial cover sheets were printed with the £5.99 price, and that the price was then changed to £4.99, with additional cover sheets printed. It seems likely the copies priced at £5.99 are therefore the true first state of the first edition (although, paradoxically, they seem more abundant than copies priced at £4.99).

A1f - United Kingdom: HarperCollins 1998 - mass market paperback priced at £6.99, ISBN: 0006512666. Approximatey 6000 copies printed.

A1g - as "Avance Rapide" - France: Pocket 1998 - paperback priced at 37FF, ISBN: 226607895X. Translated by Gregoire Dannereau.

A1h - as "Ciudad" - Spain: Mondadori 2000 - paperback, ISBN: 8439702906. Translated by Josè Manuel Pomares.

A1i - United States: Bantam 2000 - paperback original priced at $6.50, ISBN: 0553579703. Cover art by Chris Moore. First US edition.
    A1ii - Proof copy in plain red wraps.

A1j - United States: Science Fiction Book Club 2000 - hardcover, unpriced, ISBN: 0780739413920, SFBC code 33392. Same cover art as **A1i**. First hardcover edition.

A1k - as "Fremad, Kun Fremad" - Denmark: Modtryk 2000 - trade paperback, ISBN: 8439702906. Translated by Jan Mølgaard.

A1l - as "Stark, Der Traumdetektiv" - Germany: Rowholt 2001 - paperback, ISBN: 3499229471.

A1m - Japan: Sony Magazines 2001 - hardcover priced at ¥2000.00, ISBN: 4789717283. Translated by Yoichi Shimada.

A1n - United States: Subterranean Press 2002. Released in two limited states with cover art and internal illustrations by Zaz Kee.
    A1nn - Proof copy in wraps.
    A1n.1 - Limited edition - 750 signed, numbered hardcover copies bound in cloth, with dustjacket, priced at $40.00, ISBN: 1931081115.
    A1n.2 - Lettered edition - 26 signed, lettered copies in traycase, priced at $250.00.

A1o - United Kingdom: HarperCollins 2002 - mass market paperback priced at £7.99, ISBN: 0007127758. Issued as part of the "Voyager Classics" series.

A2 SPARES

"As noted elsewhere, **Spares** came about through a collision between an image I'd long had knocking about in my head (that of cloned people stumbling silently in a blue tunnel), with a request for a short story for a themed anthology - Stephen Jones' **Mammoth Book of Frankenstein**. I wrote the short story almost in one sitting. By the time I'd got to the end, I'd started to wonder whether it might form the basis of a novel.

"**To Receive is Better** is 3000 words long. **Spares** is 118,000. The difference between the two is 115,000 words - the length of **Only Forward**.

"115,000 words, I rapidly discovered, don't grow on trees. Whereas **Only Forward** had largely come to me of its own volition, the early parts of **Spares** had to be hacked out of the word mines syllable by syllable. They often say that second novels are the hardest, and I'm here to tell you that they're right. Especially when you've just decided to become a full-time writer and you have no idea of the discipline that entails...

"When I got past the first few chapters, however, things started getting a little easier. Sometimes it can be that way: you end up polishing and polishing an early section of something, trying to work up the escape velocity to break forward into the rest of the book, to the point where your first chapter looms so large in your own mind that it's impossible to believe there might even be anything after it. In the end, after a few months of wailing and gnashing of teeth, I took the extreme step of lopping the whole first chapter off, cutting most of the second and third, and starting again. This didn't quite reduce me to nothing - I'd worked out a few small parts of the later sections of the story in the meantime - and it did have the effect of freeing me up to get going on them. Not least because of deadline panic, I suspect: 'Yesterday I had twenty thousand words, and now I've got five thousand. This is really not going well...'

"In the end I was pleased with the book, especially after one of my editors - Jim Rickards - had kicked me into some extensive rewriting on a later chapter. I had started reading a lot of crime in that period, and the influence of James Ellroy, Jim Thompson and James Lee Burke is probably there for those who want to find it. Also important were the usual little events in 'real' life: the twenty years of a recurring dream of being in something very like a MegaMall; a vacation in New Orleans (the inspiration for some of the 8th floor of New Richmond); some interesting recreational experiences; this and that. For those who want to find out more, The Overlook Connection's Limited Edition of **Spares** has the following additional material: the cut first chapter, a short piece citing a few more real-life sources for some of the ideas, and four short stories (one otherwise unpublished, and another hard to get hold of) that contain some seeds for the novel.

"The months after finishing **Spares** marked a fairly major change in my life. After a good sale to an American publisher, and the novel's optioning by Stephen Speilberg's DreamWorks SKG, being a full-time writer seemed a slightly less precarious position.

"As to its film position now, ask the magic eight ball: The Future Is Uncertain, but as of December 2003, the book is under option by Paramount."

A2a - United Kingdom: HarperCollins 1996 - hardcover priced at £9.99, ISBN: 0002246562. Two print runs, the first (with complete number line starting with a one) approximately 3000 copies, the second only 1000.

    A2aa - Proof copy in pink illustrated wraps. 450 copies printed.

    A2aaa - Promotional postcards. Four variants, reproducing the cover of **A2a** with a brief message on each - see below. These were free postcards given away at pubs and cinemas.

    A2aaa.1 - "What do I know? I'm just a fucking fridge".

    A2aaa.2 - "Tune in/Turn on/Fuck Off".

    A2aaa.3 - "Fucked up? You will be".

    A2aaa.4 - "Available in all good bookshops. And some really shit ones".

A2b - United Kingdom: Waterstones 1996 - extract in "The Alien Has Landed" issue 5. Edited by Ariel. In-house magazine produced by Waterstones Deansgate, Manchester.

A2c - United Kingdom: HarperCollins 1996 - trade paperback, unpriced, no barcode on back, same cover as **A2a**, same ISBN number. Either a book club or an export edition.

A2d - United Kingdom: HarperCollins 1997 - mass market paperback, priced at £5.99, ISBN: 0586217754. Same cover art as **A2a**. Approximately 20,000 copies printed.

    A2dd - Promotional postcard. Reproduces the cover of **A2a**, with the text "Spares/Michael Marshall Smith/A Novel" and a blurb from David Baddiel.

A2e - United States: Bantam 1997 - hardcover priced at $22.95, ISBN: 055310604X. First US edition.
    A2ee - Proof copy in illustrated wraps.
    A2eee - Author's presentation copy. A unique leather-bound edition given by the publisher to the author.

A2f - as "Ricambi" - Italy: Gazanti 1997 - hardcover priced at L32,000.00, ISBN: 8811662990. Translated by Gianni Pannofino.

A2g - as "Clones" - Spain: Grijalbo 1997 - trade paperback, ISBN: 8425331625. Translated by Marìa Vidal.

A2h - as "Vervangers" - Holland: Luitingh 1997 - trade paperback, ISBN: 9024503361. Translated by Hugo & Nienke Kuipers.

A2i - as "Supeahzu" - Japan: Sony Magazines 1997 - hardcover priced at ¥1900, ISBN: 4789712508. Translated by Yoichi Shimada, book design by Hiroshi Hanamura, endpapers illustrated by Takashi Torao.

A2j - United Kingdom: HarperCollins 1998 - mass market paperback priced at £6.99, ISBN: 0006512674. Re-issued with new cover art. Three print runs totalling approximately 10,000 copies.

A2k - United States: Bantam 1998 - mass market paperback priced at $6.50, ISBN: 0553579010.

A2l - as "Ricambi" - Italy: Euroclub 1998 - hardcover, unpriced, no ISBN. Translated by Gianni Pannofino. Book club edition.

A2m - as "Clones" - Spain: Círculo de Lectores 1998 - hardcover, unpriced, ISBN: 8422669749. Translated by Marìa Vidal. Book club edition.

A2n - as "Geklont" - Germany: Rowholt 1998 - hardcover priced at 39.80DM, ISBN: 349806323. Translated by Ulrika Becker and Claus Varrelman.

A2o - as"Stumper" - Denmark: Forlaget Modtryck 1998 - paperback, ISBN: 8773945064. Translated by Jack Bacher.

A2p - as "Frere De Chair" - France: Calmann-Lévy 1998 - paperback priced at FF130, ISBN: 2702129099. Translated by Hèlëne Collon.

A2q - as "Klonoi" - Greece: Medusa 1998 - paperback, unpriced, ISBN: 9607014413.

A2r - as "Ricambi" - Italy: Garzanti Elefanti 1999 - paperback, ISBN: 8811668921. Translated by Gianni Pannofino.

A2s - as "Geklont" - Germany: Taschenbuch 1999 - paperback priced at 12.90DM, ISBN: 3499226995. Translated by Ulrika Becker and Claus Varrelman.

A2t - as "Frere De Chair" - France: Pocket 1999 - paperback priced at FF39, ISBN: 2266086065. Translated by Hèlëne Collon, cover art by W. Siudmak.

A2u - as "Zmieniaki" - Poland: Rebis 1999 - paperback priced at 25Zl, ISBN: 8371206194. Translated by Krzysztof Fordonski.

A2v - United States: Overlook Connection Press 1999. Released in three limited states. Introduction by Neil Gaiman, cover art by Alan M. Clark, Contains stories **B13**, **B14** and **B35**. All copies signed by the contributors.
    A2vv - Proof copy in red wraps. 20 copies produced.
    A2v.1 - Limited trade edition - 500 hardcover copies priced at $45.00, ISBN: 0963339761.
    A2v.2 - Sterling edition - 100 slipcased hardcover copies priced at $85.00, ISBN: 0963339753.
    A2v.3 - Lettered edition - 52 leather-bound, traycased hardcover copies priced at $350.00. ISBN: 096333977X. Issued without dust jacket.

A2w - as "Clones" - Spain: Grijalbo 2000 - paperback, ISBN: 9700508943. Translated by Marìa Vidal.

A2x - as "Náhradníci" - Czech Republic: BB-Art 1999 - hardcover priced at Kc196.00, ISBN: 8072571206. Translated by Eva Poskocilova.

A2y - as "Clones" - Portugal: Notias Editorial 2000 - paperback, ISBN 972460956.

A2z - as "Chalufyim" - Israel: Aryeh Nir 2001 - paperback priced at NIS74.00, no ISBN. Translated by Inga Michaeli.

A2*a - as "Supeahzu" - Japan: Sony Magazines 2001 - paperback priced at

¥840.00, ISBN: 4789717674. Translated by Yoichi Shimada.

A2*b - as "Avance Rapide" - France: Bragelonne 2002 - trade paperback priced at €20.00, ISBN: 2914370229. Translated by Ange, cover artwork by Alain Janolle.
    A2*bb - bookmark reproducing the cover.

A3 WHEN GOD LIVED IN KENTISH TOWN

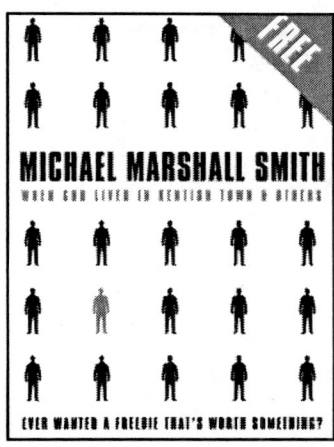

"This very tiny volume was basically a promotional item developed between my publishers and a division of WHSmith, collecting just four stories - **When God lived in Kentish Town**, **Diet Hell**, **Everybody Goes** *and* **Save As...**

"The book was designed to be given away free in the WHSmith branches associated with their travel retail division - in major UK train stations and airports, basically. It was actually rather a long time before I saw one myself, as I didn't have occasion to go anywhere long distance at that time, but luckily Steve Jones eventually managed to grab me a couple from Heathrow.

"I like it. It's a cute little book, and the stories aren't bad, and for three out of four to be previously-unpublished isn't too shabby either. I suspect a lot were grabbed by manic home-bound commuters and then left on the train at the other end, but hopefully a few nudged people into taking a risk on the whole collection."

A3a - United Kingdom: HarperCollins 1998 - paperback, unpriced, no ISBN. Containing stories **B21**, **B29**, **B30**, **B34**. 5000 copies printed.

michael marshall smith
an annotated bibliography

A4 ONE OF US

"The central idea of **One of Us** - that of a man who caretakes other people's memories - came out of a dream. I dreamt that I was in my bed, and had just woken up: at which point I turned to a small machine at my beside, to see how many dreams I'd just had for other people. And then I woke up again, into what I assume is the real world. As noted under **The Dark Land**, the dreams I find weirdest and most memorable are the ones in which I dream of myself being in exactly the same position that I am in reality. Dreaming that I'm asleep in my bed? What the hell is the point of that?

"So I remembered the dream-logging dream, and soon realised that substituting memories for dreams might take the idea somewhere interesting. This gave rise to a short story called **REMtemps**. Whereas I didn't really begin thinking about a novel based on **To Receive is Better** until I'd finished the story, with **REMtemps** I was thinking about it before I was halfway through. As a result the short story goes off slightly half-cocked, and has never been published. I just tucked it in a folder on the hard disk, rolled up my sleeves, and got typing.

"Compared with **Spares**, **One of Us** was a much easier ride. I had a bunch of ideas floating around ready for it, and a number of compelling coincidences (dreams and coincidences - I sound a real space cadet, I know: but actually I'm hard as nails) pushed me into the book with a strong following wind. I was a little more experimental with structure than before, and there were a few parts where I have to admit I had no idea what was going to happen next, but in general it was fun. I know that some people don't like the last chapter, with its ontological and metaphysical flight of fancy, but you know what? I don't care. I like that part. And it's my book. And yes I had the idea for that part before I started, and yes I know it's a deus ex machina: that's the whole point.

"The usual real life components; there is a bar called Houssons in Ensinada, and it's good fun if you're in a hectic frame of mind; I did spend a little while in Santa Monica during that period (but then made up most of the geography); and I really do hate being massaged.

"**One of Us** was optioned within a few weeks of completion, by Di Novi Pictures and Heyday Films for Warner Brothers. Over the next three years five or six scripts were written, and they seemed to be getting very close, but in the end the *project floundered. The Future? Ask Again Later."*

A4a - United Kingdom: HarperCollins 1998 - hardcover priced at £14.99, ISBN: 0002256002. One print run of 5000 copies.
>   **A4aa** - Proof copy in illustrated white wraps. 450 copies printed. Proof jackets were also produced, bearing a £12.99 price.
>   **A4aaa** - Promotional postcard - a fold-over postcard reproducing the cover of **A4a**, with additional material on rear.

A4b - United Kingdom: HarperCollins 1998 - trade paperback, unpriced, no barcode on back, same cover as **A4a**, same ISBN number. Either a book club or an export edition.

A4c - United Kingdom: HarperCollins 1998 - extract in "GQ Anthology of New Fiction" - paperback, unpriced, ISBN: 0583452809. A slim promotional paperback distributed with GQ Magazine.

A4d - United States: Bantam 1998 - hardcover priced at $23.95, ISBN: 0553106058. First US edition.
>   **A4dd** - Proof copy in illustrated wraps.
>   **A4ddd** - Author's presentation copy. A unique leather-bound edition given by the publisher to the author.

A4e - as "Uno Di Noi" - Italy: Garzanti Libri 1998 - hardcover priced at L32,000 ISBN: 8811662524. Translated by Gianni Pannofino.

A4f - as "Onder Ons" - Holland: Luitingh 1998 - trade paperback, unpriced, ISBN: 9024514975. Translated by Hugo & Nienke Kuipers.

A4g - as "Suenos" - Spain: Grijalbo 1998 - hardcover, unpriced, ISBN: 8425332842. Translated by Josè Manuel Pomares.

A4h - as "Wan Oyu Asu" - Japan: Sony Magazines 1998 - hardcover priced at ¥1800, ISBN: 4789714187. Translated by Yoichi Shimada, jacket design by Hiroshi Hanamura, jacket illustration by Toru Kageyama.

A4i - as "Suenos" - Spain: Círculo De Lectores 1999 - hardcover, unpriced, ISBN: 8422678691. Translated by Josè Manuel Pomares. Book club edition.

A4j - United Kingdom: HarperCollins 1999 - mass market paperback priced at

£6.99, ISBN: 000649997X. Approximately 35,000 copies printed.

A4k - United States: Bantam 1999 - mass market paperback priced at $6.50, ISBN: 0553580698.

A4l - as "R.E.M" - Germany: Rowohlt 1999 - hardcover, ISBN: 3498044001. Translated by Thomas Stregers and Claus Varrelman.

A4m - as "Memorias Que Matan" - Portugal: Notícias Editorial 1999 - ISBN: 924610349. Translated by Pedro Dias.

A4n - as "La Proie Des Reves" - France: Calmann-Lévy 1999 - trade paperback priced at FF130, ISBN: 2702130186. Translated by Hèlëne Collon.

A4o - as "Jeden z Nas" - Czech Republic: BB-Art 1999 - hardcover priced at Kc185.00, ISBN: 8072570498.

A4p - as "La Proie des Reves" - France: Pocket SF 2001 - paperback priced at FF48.45, ISBN : 2266098039. Translated by Hèlëne Collon, cover art by W. Siudmak.

A4q - as "Jeden z Nas" - Poland: Rebis 2001 - paperback priced at 28Zl, ISBN: 837120941X. Translated by Wieslaw Marcysiak.

A5 WHAT YOU MAKE IT

"I'd been looking forward for years to putting a collection together, partly because - after a few years' hard novel writing - it seemed like a cool idea to be able to produce another book without creating the whole thing from scratch, but mainly because I just liked the idea of the stories collected together. I've always loved reading and writing short stories, and the notion of pulling mine out of the various anthologies, magazines and chapbooks and giving them a hardbacked home of their own was very appealing.

"The actual process was a lot harder than I was expecting. The first problem was choosing the stories. Some were obvious inclusions: the award-winners, and a few others which had been picked up for a fistful of 'Best Of' anthologies. Then there were less celebrated ones I just happened to have a particular affection for, and finally some which hadn't been published at all. Once they were gathered together, however, it became obvious that some didn't sit as well in a group as they had individually, and overall balance had to be considered. Then there was the question of length. The 'first draft' of the collection, a list of stories put together by my editor and I, would have come in at nearly twice the final length. While this would have been nice for me, and I hope for the people who like my work, it wouldn't have made much publishing sense. Fans of genre fiction tend to be unusually fond of short stories, because experience tells them that a lot of good horror and science fiction comes in this form. The general public, to whom the book would be marketed, remain less convinced. They'll buy this season's slim volume of mannered little pieces from the literary flavour-of-the-month, but a huge great tome from some genre yahoo just isn't going to be their thing. They'd rather have a novel, thank you, something they can really get their teeth into while sipping fruity cocktails and sitting by the pool.

"So we cut out a bunch of stories, one effect of which was that there is a little less previously unpublished material than I would have liked. In fact, apart from a very short poem right at the end, the only completely new stuff was **Diet Hell, Everybody Goes, When God Lived in Kentish Town** and the title story, **What You Make It.** I liked these stories, however, and they had a freshness which comes from never having seen them printed in another anthology, so I hope the balance worked out okay. Given the reduced rate at which I seem to be producing short fiction these days, it's actually quite a few to go out in one shot.

"I'd always assumed the collection would be called **The Man Who Drew Cats and Other Stories**, but when they'd read the story I'd written specially for the collection, both my wife and editor agreed its title should become that of the whole book."

A5a - United Kingdom: HarperCollins 1999 - hardcover priced at £12.99, ISBN: 0002256029. One print run of 5000 copies.

> **A5aa** - Proof copy - Spiral-bound A4 pages produced in-house. Reportedly only 20 copies produced.

A5b - United Kingdom: HarperCollins 2000 - mass market paperback priced at £6.99, ISBN: 0006510078. Approximately 15,000 copies printed.

A5c - as "Cuerpos Ajenos" - Spain: Plaza Janés 2003 - trade paperback priced at € 16.50, ISBN: 8401315751. Translated by Rita da Costa.

A6 THE VACCINATOR

"Though quite a few of my short stories are quite long, especially the ones of a few years ago, I'd never tried swapping up a weight to the full-fledged novella. But I'd already had the idea about a man arranging a special type of kidnapping vaccine, and when Peter Crowther invited me to do a novella for a new series he was setting up with PS Publishing, I was happy to give it a try.

"I enjoyed it. Twenty thousand words is a nice length, short enough to let you settle down into the story and characters without fear of going over-length, but not so long that you have to start getting too heavy with back story and overall structure. It was also nice to write something in the third person again, with the freedom that yields for alternate viewpoints, and I also pared down the prose style a little. Both of these experiments probably contributed to the texture of my next novel, **The Straw Men**.

"The novella is set in Key West because I'd just been on honeymoon there, and two of the characters in the story could be said to reflect that. When my wife read the story she was lightly scandalised at seeing her recent past alluded to in a work of fiction.

"'Well hey,' I said, turning slowly. 'Remember the girls in the short stories. At least you get to live...'"

A6a - United Kingdom: PS Publishing 1999. Released in two limited states. Introduction by M. John Harrison, jacket design by Simon Turner, interior design by Simon Conway.

> **A6a.1** - 500 paperback copies, unpriced, ISBN: 1902880064. Black and white cover, signed by MMS. Although unpriced, copies retailed at £8.00.
>
> **A6a.2** - 150 hardcover copies, unpriced, ISBN: 1902880072. Issued with full-colour dustjacket, signed by MMS and MJH. Although unpriced, copies retailed at £25.00.

A6b - in "Foursight" - United Kingdom: Gollancz 2000 - hardcover priced at £16.99, ISBN: 0575068701. A collection of four novellas previously published by PS Publishing.

A6c - in "Binary 2" - United Kingdom: Millenium 2000 - mass market paperback priced at £4.99, ISBN: 1857987608. A back-to-back edition, bound together with Kim Newman's **Andy Warhol's Dracula**.

A6d - as "Vaccinator" - in "Faux Reveur" - France: Bragelonne 2002 - trade paperback priced at €22.00 , ISBN: 2914370156. Translated by Ange, cover art by David Oghia. An anthology comprising the first eight novellas issued by PS Publishing.

A6e - Appeared in **A9**.

A7 CAT STORIES

*"I'd been talking to Paul Miller of Earthling Publications for a while about us possibly doing something together, when Paul found the great Patti Kaufman illustration that was used for the cover of this mini-anthology. Paul suggested that we reprint two of my previous cat-featuring stories (**The Man Who Drew Cats, Not Waving**) and that I write a new one to round it off. Good idea, I thought - and was finally able to write a story (**They Also Serve**) around one of my most long-standing ideas. The book was a really enjoyable experience to put together, as Paul is one of the most professional people I've ever dealt with, and I'm very happy with the end package."*

A7a - United States: Earthling Publications 2001. Released in two limited states. Short story collection containing **B1, B20, B42**. Introduction by MMS, cover art by Patti Kaufman.

    A7aa - Proof copy - 4 bound copies of galley proofs, signed by MMS and publisher Paul Miller.*

    A7a.1 - 350 numbered copies, staple-bound in colour wraps, priced at $13.00, no ISBN. signed by MMS.

    A7a.2 - 15 lettered, traycased, cloth-bound hardcover copies, priced at $200.00, no ISBN. Includes original cat sketch by MMS and a facsimile of the original, hand-written manuscript of **B1** (see **B1k**). Signed by MMS and PK.

    A7a.3 - An additional third state, not offered for sale, comprising a small number of presentation hardcover copies in slipcase. Unpriced, no ISBN. Signed by MMS and PK.

---

* There were also two A5-sized printer proofs produced for reference purposes

A8 THE STRAW MEN *(as by MICHAEL MARSHALL)*

"To say that **The Straw Men** is the most difficult book I've written would be putting it very, very mildly. There were a number of reasons for this. The first was that I had decided that, having written three novels that can probably be best described as science fiction, I wanted to do something else for this one. This was partly because I wanted to pull my novel and short story writing a little closer together - and have very seldom written sf short stories - and partly because I felt that I was ready for something else. The second complicating factor was that during the period of writing **The Straw Men** I had to contend with any number of other pieces of work with screaming deadlines - notably a couple of drafts of **Modesty Blaise** which I did for Wandering Star and Miramax.

"It was a hard book to write, too. Much of the material was in my head already - the underlying idea, the characters, and a good deal of the stuff on serial killers, in which I have been interested for many years. Making the transition to the present day wasn't actually that hard - though I missed being able to make up so much stuff. The tough thing was getting it all to work together, and creating an ending which paid off all the things it needed to. It took a long time, and several attempts, before my editors and I were happy.

"I think now that it's probably the best thing I've ever done. I'm writing this before it's been published, however, so time will tell whether or not anyone else agrees..."

A8a - United States: Jove 2002 - paperback priced at $6.99, ISBN: 0515134279.
    A8aa - Proof copy in illustrated wraps.

A8b - United Kingdom: HarperCollins 2002 - hardcover priced at £10.00, ISBN: 002256010. First printing with yellow endpapers, second printing with brown endpapers. Approximately 15,000 copies printed. Wrap-around band attached stating: "as addictive as John Connolly or your money back".
    A8bb - The proof copy in wraps. This is, in fact, the true first state of the novel, preceding the US proof by several weeks, and the only state to carry the author's name as Michael Marshall Smith. Several copies available with proof dust jackets also carrying the

author's full name.

A8c - United Kingdom: HarperCollins 2002 - trade paperback, unpriced, no ISBN. Book club edition, with code CN 106323.

A8d - United Kingdom: HarperCollins 2002 - trade paperback, unpriced, ISBN: 0007151861. Export edition, thicker than **A8c** although similar in format.

A8e - United Kingdom: HarperCollins 2003 - mass market paperback priced at £6.99, ISBN: 0006499988
  A8ee - the proof copy in wraps. Unpriced, with "Free Advance Edition" on front, marketing material on back.

A9 MORE TOMORROW & OTHER STORIES

"Apart from the cover (which I didn't like much at all) I was quite pleased with the first gathering of my stories in **What You Make It**; but - as noted - would have liked to include a few more. Well, with this collection, we sure as hell have. I had been approached over the years by a couple of publishers to do an American version, as **What You Make It** wasn't really available in the US, and there had been a few stories since (notably the novella **The Vaccinator**) which I thought it would be nice to put into a collection. I had previously worked with Paul Miller of Earthling on the small **Cat Stories** volume, and very pleased to be dealing with him again. We came up with a list of stories which, though not actually exhaustive, is pretty damned comprehensive, and I agreed to produce four new ones for the collection. These, plus the proportion not available except in the original published form, make it a significantly different book to the previous one - though there is some common ground.

"There's an introduction by my friend and mentor Stephen Jones, and an afterword which I wrote in the response to the question 'Who do you write short stories?'

"The book was a pleasure to work on from start to finish. Paul is very particular about his art, and he went to great lengths to find an artist we both liked. I think John Picacio's cover art and design looks very good indeed - and I'm looking forward to having a finished copy in my hand! "

A9a - United States: Earthling Publications 2003. Released in two limited states. Introduction by Stephen Jones, afterword by Smith, cover artwork by John Picacio, interior design by Paul Miller.
  A9aa - The proof in blue wraps. 21 copies produced, of which ten were

signed on a special limitation sheet and housed in a black handmade slipcase.

A9a.1 - 1000 numbered hardcover copies priced at $40.00, ISBN: 0974420301. Signed by Smith.

A9a.2 - 26 lettered leather-bound, traycased hardcover copies priced at $250.00, signed by Smith, Jones and Picacio. Includes separate bonus piece, "Happy Holidays", a fictional holiday letter from the Smith family.

michael marshall smith
an annotated bibliography

Limited Editions

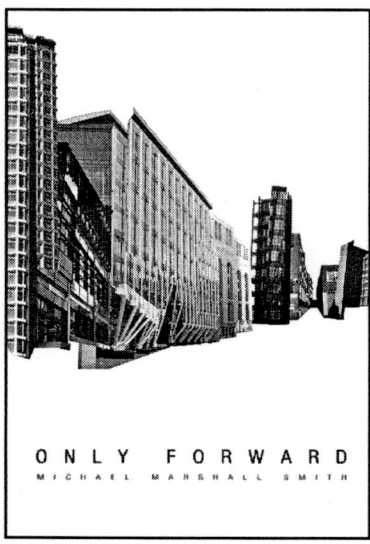

UK First Editions

MICHAEL
MARSHALL SMITH
ONLY FORWARD

spares
michael marshall smith
"Shocking, moving and surreal"
CLIVE BARKER

MICHAEL MARSHALL SMITH ONE OF US
EVER DONE ANYTHING YOU'D LIKE TO FORGET?
THE THRILLER HAS JUST EVOLVED

MICHAEL
MARSHALL
SPECIAL PRICE £10
AS ADDICTIVE AS
JOHN CONNOLLY
OR YOUR MONEY BACK
THE
STRAW
MEN
Friends. Neighbours. Serial killers.

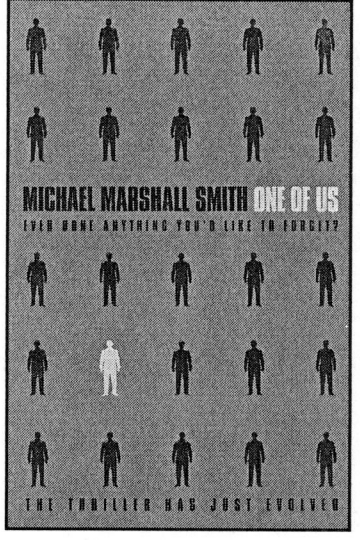

B Short Stories

B1 THE MAN WHO DREW CATS

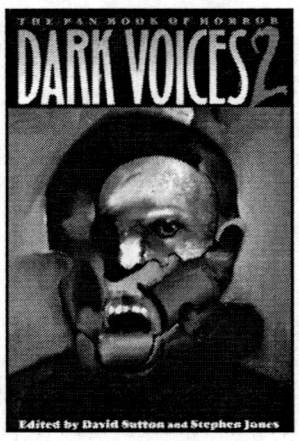

"During the summer of 1987 I was on tour around Britain with the Cambridge Footlights - the university group that gave rise to Monty Python and many subsequent English comedy stalwarts. The tour schlepped around all over the country for three months, from Leatherhead to Plymouth to Harrogate and Nottingham and God knows where in between. I had just discovered Stephen King at the time, and spent my spare moments, of which there were a great many, devouring everything of his I could find. I latched onto him rather later than the rest of the world, but luckily this meant there was a huge backlog for me to catch up on. I might not have discovered him at all but for a suggestion from my friend Howard Ely: after years of my badgering him to read Kingsley Amis' **Lucky Jim**, he finally relented one evening in a pub - on the condition that I read **The Talisman** by King and Peter Straub. I dutifully went out and bought it, and settled down with a sceptically-raised eyebrow - having not read any contemporary horror fiction. I was hooked, and have been ever since. Without King I might never have become a writer, and so if you want to blame anyone, Howard's squarely in the frame. He liked **Lucky Jim** too, so that worked out nicely.

"The Footlights tour ended with a two-week stint at the Edinburgh Fringe, playing the graveyard shift at the Assembly Rooms. The days were free, and instead of wasting them watching twelve different productions of **The Accidental Death of an Anarchist**, I spent them wandering around Edinburgh - one of the world's most beautiful cities - and drinking endless coffees in the company of King's demons and doomed heroes.

"One particular afternoon near the end of our run I was sitting on the steps of the big gallery at The Mound. Some distance away a man was painting a huge picture on the ground with chalks, and nearby a young child started crying wretchedly - I don't know why. From these two chance events came the idea for **The Man Who Drew Cats**, the first story I ever completed. Stephen Jones and David Sutton bought it for **Dark Voices 2**, their re-launch of the seminal **Pan Books of Horror**, and it went on to win the British Fantasy Awards for best Short

Story and Best Newcomer. This attracted the attention of my publisher, and the rest, as they say, is geography. Had I taken a different turn on that day, gone for a different walk or sat facing in a different direction, none of that would have happened. Other stuff might have, but not that. This might not have made much of a difference to many people's lives, but it sure as hell would have to mine. I don't know about you, but fate scares the shit out of me.

"By the way: anyone who thinks my primary influence of the time might be rather evident should check out the names of the two towns mentioned in the story. I knew it too."

B1a - Dark Voices 2: The Pan Book of Horror - United Kingdom: Pan 1990 - paperback priced at £3.99, ISBN: 0330313738. Edited by Stephen Jones & David Sutton.

B1b - Dark Voices 2 - United Kingdom: Severn House 1991 - hardcover priced at £11.99, ISBN: 0727841963. Edited by Stephen Jones and David Sutton.

B1c - Best New Horror 2 - United Kingdom: Robinson 1991 - trade paperback priced at £7.99, ISBN: 1854870947. Edited by Stephen Jones & Ramsey Campbell.

B1d - Best New Horror 2 - United States: Carroll & Graf 1991 - hardcover priced at $20.95, ISBN: 0881847364. Edited by Stephen Jones & Ramsey Campbell.
B1dd - proof copy in wraps.

B1e - Best New Horror 2 - United States: Carroll & Graf 1993 - trade paperback priced at $11.95, ISBN: 0881849219. Edited by Stephen Jones & Ramsey Campbell.

B1f - The Giant Book of Best New Horror - United Kingdom: Magpie / Australia: The Book Company 1993 - trade paperback, ISBN: 1854871935.

B1g - The Giant Book of Best New Horror - United Kingdom: Magpie/Parragon 1993 - trade paperback, ISBN: 1858131758. Edited by Stephen Jones & Ramsey Campbell.

B1h - The Giant Book of Best New Horror - United Kingdom: Robinson 1993 - trade paperback priced at £10.95, ISBN: 1854871935. Edited by Stephen Jones and Ramsey Campbell.

B1i - Appeared in **A5**.

B1j - Appeared in **A7**.

B1k - United States: Earthling Publications 2002 - 15 lettered staple-bound copies. Facsimile of the original holograph manuscript. Produced to accompany **A7a.2**.

B1l - as "Der Mann, der Katzen zeichnete" - in "Omen, Das Horror-Journal" - Germany: Festa Verlag 2003 - paperback magazine priced at €12.95, ISBN: 3935822693.

B1m - Appeared in **A9**.

B2 THE DARK LAND

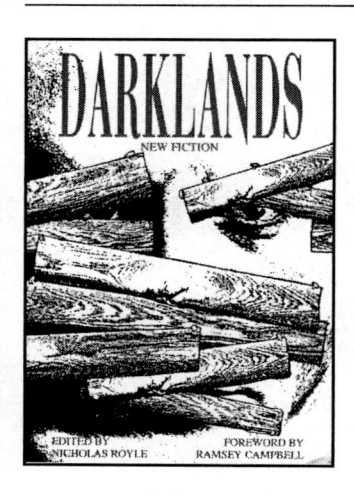

"This was another very early story, possibly the second or third I ever wrote. It came about simply enough. On a few occasions in my life, I have had a dream in which I have dreamt that I was where I actually was in reality. In this story, for example, I dreamt that I was asleep on the bed on which I was actually asleep. It's a curious kind of dream to have, because when you wake up you're extremely disorientated: am I really here now, or what? And also, what is your mind trying to tell you with this kind of dream? That you are... where you are?

The Dark Land was the first time I used a technique which I have had constant recourse to since - that of taking an idea from a dream, or even just a dream itself, writing it down and seeing where it leads me. The first section of the story, up to the point where the two weird men march into the kitchen for the first time, is a verbatim account of the dream. After that I just let it run."

B2a - Darklands - United Kingdom: Egerton Press 1992 - paperback priced at £2.95, ISBN: 0951852000. Edited by Nicholas Royle.

B2b - Best New Horror 3 - United States: Carroll & Graf 1992 - hardcover priced at $21.00, ISBN: 0881848581. Edited by Stephen Jones and Ramsey Campbell.

B2c - Best New Horror 3 - United Kingdom: Robinson 1992 - trade paperback priced at £7.99, ISBN: 1854871323. Edited by Stephen Jones and Ramsey Campbell.

B2d - Darklands - United Kingdom: Hodder & Stoughton 1993 - paperback priced at £3.99, ISBN: 0450597644. Edited by Nicholas Royle.

B2e - Best New Horror 3 - United States: Carroll & Graf 1994 - trade paperback priced at $11.95, ISBN: 0786700289. Edited by Stephen Jones and Ramsey Campbell.

B2f - The Giant Book of Terror - United Kingdom: Magpie / Australia: The Book Company 1994 - trade paperback, ISBN: 1854873768. Edited by Stephen Jones and Ramsey Campbell.

B2g - The Giant Book of Terror - United Kingdom: Parragon 1994 - trade paperback, ISBN: 0752501429. Edited by Stephen Jones and Ramsey Campbell.

B2h - Appeared in **A5**.

B2i - Appeared in **A9**.

B3 ALWAYS

"I'm an enormous fan of Christmas. It's my favourite time of year. This is a story about Christmas and love. That's all."

B3a - Darklands 2 - United Kingdom: Egerton Press 1992 - paperback priced at £4.99, ISBN: 0951852019. Edited by Nicholas Royle.

B3b - Darklands 2 - United Kingdom: NEL 1994 - paperback priced at £4.99, ISBN: 0450604365. Edited by Nicholas Royle.

B3c - The Grown-ups' Book of Books - United Kingdom: Headline 1999 - paperback priced at £1.00, ISBN: 0747260893. Published as a "sampler" for World Book Day.

B3d - appeared in **A5**.

B3e - Appeared in **A9**.

B4 A TIME FOR WAITING

"An early short. Very early, in fact, certainly one of the first five stories I wrote. The people in it are based very, very loosely on those I was working with at the time. The style is pretty old-fashioned, I suppose: but I think it kind of works. At least it's short and to the point."

B4a - Dark Voices 4 - United Kingdom: Pan 1992 - paperback priced at £4.99, ISBN: 0330324764. Edited by Stephen Jones and David Sutton.

B4b - 100 Twisted Little Tales of Torment - United States: Barnes & Noble 1998 - hardcover, unpriced, ISBN: 076070855X. Edited by Stefan Dziemianowicz, Robert Weingberg and Martin H. Greenberg. Cover artwork by Lynn Binder.

B5 THE OWNER

"Strange history for this story. I originally wrote it, many years ago, as a half hour screenplay. There was no home for it: it simply occurred to me in visual terms first, and so that's how I wrote it - reasoning that it might also serve as a kind of specimen script. Didn't do anything with it.

"Then, a little while later, Peter Crowther invited me to contribute to an anthology, and I realised that the story enshrined in the screenplay would do very well. So I converted it to a short story. I loathed the process (because I already knew what was going to happen, and I hate that), but in the end I was happy with the way

the story worked.

"Then, a few more years later, I was approached by the BBC to consider writing a one-off hour and a half drama for them. I showed the woman a few short stories, and she really liked **The Owner**. We worked for a few months to try to convert it to this format, but oddly, it didn't seem to work - and in the end we dropped it.

"Then again last year, I wasted a couple of months writing two more drafts of hour-long adaptations of the story for Channel 4, neither of which came to anything.

"I'm beginning to suspect that either (a) it's a short story and has been all along, despite the odd beginning, or (b) it can't be expanded, and any screen version of it has to stick at half an hour.

"I hope it's the latter, because now someone else is interested in adapting it for television..."

B5a - Touch Wood - United Kingdom: Little Brown 1993 - hardcover priced at £15.99, ISBN 0316-907324. Edited by Peter Crowther.

B5b - Touch Wood - United Kingdom: Warner 1994 - mass market paperback priced at £5.99, ISBN: 0751506982. Edited by Peter Crowther.

B5c - Touch Wood - United States: Warner Aspect 1996 - mass market paperback priced at $5.99, ISBN: 0446601624. Edited by Peter Crowther.

B5d - Appeared in **A5**.

B6 MORE BITTER THAN DEATH

"I wanted to write a story about a killer that took you as far inside his head as possible; that suckered you in, put you on his side, and then showed you what his world was really like. Hence this cheery little tale, which is part of what Chris Fowler has referred to as my 'dead girlfriend' cycle. There was a period a long while ago when, in one way or another, a lot of my stories seemed to feature the demise of the protagonist's loved one. It was, I'm keen to stress, nothing personal. I've stopped doing that now, more or less, to my wife's relief."

"My mother is not a huge fan of this story, for reasons which may be clear."

B6a - Dark Voices 5 - United Kingdom: Pan 1993 - paperback priced at £4.99, ISBN: 0330330241. Edited by Stephen Jones and David Sutton.

michael marshall smith
an annotated bibliography

B6b - Appeared in **A5**.

B6c - Appeared in **A9**.

B7 LATER

"The genesis of this story illustrates the serendipitous collision of trivial events which accounts for a vast proportion of the world's fiction. I had just attended a Convention in Birmingham, at which Stephen Jones mentioned he was putting together a collection entitled **The Mammoth Book of Zombies**. *Nicholas Royle gave me a lift back to London in his mad mini, and slapped Roger Waters' Amused to Death in the tape machine. The song* **Watching TV**, *which tells of how a girl was killed in a riot, affected me very strongly.*

"A day later out popped the story, fully formed. That's the way it goes - but only very, very occasionally."

B7a - The Mammoth Book of Zombies - United Kingdom: Robinson 1993 - trade paperback priced at £5.99, ISBN: 1854872281. Edited by Stephen Jones.

B7b - The Mammoth Book of Zombies - United States: Carroll & Graf 1993 - trade paperback priced at $9.95, ISBN: 0786700238. Edited by Stephen Jones.

B7c - The Best New Horror 5 - United Kingdom: Robinson 1994 - trade paperback priced at £6.99, ISBN: 1854872990. Edited by Stephen Jones and Ramsey Campbell.

B7d - The Best New Horror 5 - United States: Carroll & Graf 1994 - trade paperback priced at $9.95, ISBN: 0786701552. Edited by Stephen Jones.

B7e - The Year's Best Fantasy and Horror: Seventh Annual Collection - United States: St. Martin's Press 1994. Edited by Ellen Datlow and Terri Windling.
    B7e.1 - Hardcover priced at $26.95, ISBN: 0312111037.
    B7e.2 - Trade paperback priced at $16.95, ISBN: 0312111029.

B7f - as "Piú Tardi" in "Il Ritorno Degli Zombi" - Italy: Arnoldo Mondadori Editore 1994 - trade paperback priced at L9000, ISBN: 9771120496011. Edited by Stephen Jones.

B7g - The Giant Book of Zombies - United Kingdom: Magpie / Australia: The Book Company 1995 - trade paperback, ISBN: 1854876104. Edited by Stephen Jones.

B7h - The Giant Book of Zombies - United Kingdom: Parragon 1995 - trade paperback priced at £2.99, ISBN: 0752510304. Edited by Stephen Jones.

B7i - Appeared in **A5**.

B7j - Appeared in **A9**.

B8 THE FRACTURE

"I am, I have to admit, slightly prey to obsessive behaviour. Not to the point of needing medication, but certainly enough to require that I make very sure that doors are locked (see **The Owner**) *and that cigarette butts are well and truly out before leaving the house. Actually, I'm a bit more relaxed on the subject now than when I wrote the story, but the tendency's still there. For a long time I tried to work out where this kind of behaviour came from, and one of my theories was that within my head there were a number of people, some of whom performed certain acts and paid attention to them; others of which missed the event (through being temporarily dormant), and therefore weren't convinced it had happened. This story is a kind of development of this idea. It's also an example of the kind of trouble you can get into through using your imagination. The main character in this story has both a girlfriend and a mistress. I didn't. Try explaining that to your girlfriend."*

B8a - Dark Voices 6: The Pan Book of Horror - United Kingdom: Pan 1994 - mass market paperback priced at £5.99, ISBN: 0330335057. Edited by Stephen Jones and David Sutton.

B8b - Appeared in **A5**.

B9 THE VIEW

"Ah, Northwood Hall. The locale for this story is real, a massive apartment block up near Highgate in North London. I visited it once with two other guys who I was sharing a flat with, when we were looking for somewhere new to live. We... didn't end up living in Northwood Hall. Some places just have a really strange atmosphere. This place certainly did. Not a very cheerful story."

B9a - The Anthology of Fantasy & the Supernatural - United Kingdom: Tiger 1994 - hardcover priced at £9.95, ISBN: 1855015021. Edited by Stephen Jones and David Sutton.

B9b - The Giant Book of the Supernatural - United Kingdom: Magpie 1996 - trade paperback, ISBN: 1854876198. Edited by Stephen Jones and David Sutton.

B9c - The Giant Book of the Supernatural - United Kingdom: Parragon 1996 - trade paperback priced at £2.99, ISBN: 0752518445. Edited by Stephen Jones and David Sutton.

B10 AUTUMN

"Autumn is far and away my favourite season, but I have no idea how this story came about. It's a very early one, and probably had its genesis in little more than a melancholy September afternoon."

B10a - Peeping Tom - United Kingdom: Stuart Hughes 1994 - magazine priced at £2.10, issue #16 (October).

B11 TO SEE THE SEA

*"I like certain HP Lovecraft stories very much indeed, and when I was invited to contribute a modern take on the **Shadow Over Innsmouth** story I leapt at the chance. Mumbles, where the story is set, is a genuine little town on the Welsh coast, where my new girlfriend (now my wife) and I had recently spent a weekend. I'd previously been there for a friend's wedding, and actually did walk out into the mud with an old college friend of mine, both of us profoundly drunk. She managed to save her shoes. Mine were a write-off, and so I left them there."*

B11a - Shadows Over Innsmouth - United States: Fadogan & Bremer 1994. Released in two limited states. Edited by Stephen Jones.
> **B11a.1** - Trade edition - 2000 hardcover copies priced at $27.00, ISBN: 1878252186.
> **B11a.2** - Limited edition - 100 numbered, slipcased hardcover copies priced at $95.00, ISBN: 1878252194. Signed by all contributors.

B11b - Shadows Over Innsmouth - United Kingdom: Gollancz 1997 - trade paperback priced at £9.99, ISBN: 0575065729. Edited by Stephen Jones.

B11c - Shadows Over Innsmouth - United States: Del Rey 2001 - paperback priced at $14.00, ISBN 0345444078. Edited by Stephen Jones.

B11d - Shadows Over Innsmouth - Japan: Gakken 2001 - paperback priced at ¥730.00, ISBN: 4059000795. Edited by Stephen Jones. Second of two volumes.

B11e - as "Blicks auf Meer" - in "Der Cthulhu-Mythos 1976 - 2002" - Germany: Festa Verlag 2003 - hardcover priced at €20.00, ISBN: 3935822529. Edited by Frank Festa.

B11f - Appeared in **A9**.

B12 RAIN FALLS

*"This story came about through two evenings spent in a pub in Camden, North London. On the first, a fight did break out, much as described in the story. On the second evening, several years later, I was sitting at a big table in the raised area with Paula and a number of her oldest friends. This was the first time that I'd met any of them, and through one of those unfortunate seating debacles I ended up at the far end of a long table, far away from my new love, and not ideally placed to talk to any of her friends. I have the socialising abilities of a bad-tempered rock (or did then, I'm a little better now) and whiled away the hours eavesdropping on a pair of typical Camdenites on the next table (who'd evidently met through a **Time Out** personals ad, had nothing in common except a belief in astrology, and were rapidly realising this) and coming up with this story. It passed the time."*

B12a - The Mammoth Book of Werewolves - United Kingdom: Robinson 1994 - trade paperback priced at £5.99, ISBN: 1854872680. Edited by Stephen Jones.

B12b - The Mammoth Book of Werewolves - United States: Carroll & Graf 1994 - trade paperback priced at $9.95, ISBN: 0786700874. Edited by Stephen Jones.

B12c - The Giant Book of Werewolves - United Kingdom: Magpie / Australia: The Book Company 1995 - trade paperback, ISBN: 1854876090. Edited by Stephen Jones.

B12d - The Giant Book of Werewolves - United Kingdom: Parragon 1995 - trade paperback priced at £2.99, ISBN: 0752510258. Edited by Stephen Jones.

B12e - The Year's Best Fantasy and Horror: Eighth Annual Collection - United States: St. Martin's Press 1995. Edited by Ellen Datlow and Terri Windling.
    B12e.1 - Hardcover priced at $27.95, ISBN: 0312132204.
    B12e.2 - Trade paperback priced at $16.95, ISBN: 0312132190.

B12f - as "Scende la pioggia" - in "Lupi Mannari!" - Italy: Newton & Compton

1997 - trade paperback priced at L7900, ISBN: 888183801X. Edited by Stephen Jones.

B13 TO RECEIVE IS BETTER

"A long while ago, possibly as long as 15 years, I was travelling on the tube in London and suddenly experienced a flash of imagery in my mind. Blue light; a tunnel; people standing around in the claustrophobic twilight, or shambling forward. Don't know where it came from, but very soon afterwards came the idea: they're clones. They're clones of people out in the real world, and they're being stored there until needed.

"I wasn't even a writer at the time, so I didn't do anything with the idea. I remembered it, however, and seven or so years ago, when Stephen Jones asked me for a story for his upcoming **Mammoth Book Of Frankenstein**, *I realised here was a chance to use it. The story came out fast, and before I'd even finished it I'd begun to wonder whether it might form a basis for my second novel, something I was rather late on starting.*

"It did. It became **Spares**.

"On a mildly interesting note, my following novel **One of Us** *also came about through writing a short story and realising it could be expanded. The* **One of Us** *story - which was called* **REMtemps** *- has never been published."*

B13a - The Mammoth Book of Frankenstein - United Kingdom: Robinson 1994 - trade paperback priced at £5.99, ISBN: 185487330X. Edited by Stephen Jones.

B13b - The Mammoth Book of Frankenstein - United States: Carroll & Graf 1994 - trade paperback priced at $9.95, ISBN: 0786701595. Edited by Stephen Jones.

B13c - The Giant Book of Frankenstein - United Kingdom: Magpie / Australia: The Book Company 1995 - trade paperback, ISBN: 1854876112. Edited by Stephen Jones.

B13d - Best New Horror 6 - United Kingdom: Raven 1995 - trade paperback priced at £6.99, ISBN: 1854874217. Edited by Stephen Jones.

B13e - Best New Horror 6 - United States: Carroll & Graf 1995 - trade paperback priced at $10.95, ISBN: 078670277X. Edited by Stephen Jones.

B13f - "Frankenstein no Denki" - Japan: Justsystem 1995 - hardcover, ISBN: 4883094162. Edited by Stephen Jones.

B13g - "Tutte le Storie Di Frankenstein" - Italy: Newton Compton 1996 - trade paperback priced at L6900, ISBN: 8881831996. Edited by Stephen Jones.

B13h - 100 Fiendish Little Frightmares - United States: Barnes and Noble 1997 - hardcover priced at $7.98, ISBN: 076070144X. Edited by Dziemianowicz, Weinberg, and Greenberg.

B13i - as "La Joie De Recevoir" - in "Science Fiction Magazine" - France: 13 eme Rue 1999 - magazine priced at 29FF, Number 7. The story is a tear-out 8 page black and white pamphlet.

B13j - appeared in **A2u**.

B13k - Appeared in **A9**.

B14 DYING

"This is a rarity in that it's an sf short story. The only others I've written are **Save As...** *and* **They Also Serve**. *It's where I first toyed with the idea of MegaMalls, which became one of the core environments in my novel* **Spares**.*"*

B14a - Omni - United States: Omni Publications International 1994 - magazine, volume 17, number 3 (December). Edited by Ellen Datlow.

B14b - appeared in **A2u**.

B14c - Appeared in **A9**.

B15 MORE TOMORROW

"This story came about through a complete and utter ignorance of the seedier side of the internet. It is the work of someone who has absolutely no idea about that type of thing, and is entirely based on speculation, lies, and things that disreputable friends have told me.
"Is that clear?"

B15a - Dark Terrors: The Gollancz Book of Horror - United Kingdom: Gollancz 1995 - hardcover priced at £15.99, ISBN: 0575061367. Edited by Stephen Jones and David Sutton.
    B15aa - Proof copy in wraps.

B15b - Dark Terrors - United Kingdom: Vista 1996 - mass market paperback priced at £5.99, ISBN: 0575600241.

B15c - The Best New Horror Volume Seven - United Kingdom: Raven 1996 - trade paperback priced at £6.99, ISBN: 1854874640. Edited by Stephen Jones.

B15d - The Mammoth Book of Best New Horror Volume Seven - United States: Carroll & Graf 1996 - trade paperback priced at $10.95, ISBN: 0786703725. Edited by Stephen Jones.

B15e - The Year's Best Fantasy and Horror: Ninth Annual Collection - United States: St. Martin's Press 1996 - Edited by Ellen Datlow and Terri Windling.
    B15e.1 - Hardcover priced at $27.95, ISBN: 0312144490.
    B15e.2 - Trade paperback priced at $17.99, ISBN: 0312144504.

B15f - Future Visions: Tales Beyond 2000 - United Kingdom: Gollancz 1997 - paperback, unpriced. 'Sampler' of UK genre authors, distributed by Focus Magazine.

B15g - in "Online" - Germany: Heyne Bucher 1997 - paperback priced at DM12.90, ISBN: 3453116437. Edited by Werner Heilmann.

B15h - Appeared in **A5**.

michael marshall smith
an annotated bibliography

B15i - As "A Suivre" - in "Tenebres" - France: Lueurs Mortes 1998 - magazine, number 4 (October-December). Edited by Benois Domis.

B15j - Appeared in **A9**.

B16 FOREIGN BODIES

"I am moderately proud to have been a member of what appears now to be almost recognised as an English literary tradition of the early 1990s - that of **Miserablism** (see **The BFI Companion to Horror**, ed. Kim Newman 1997). The term is believed to have been coined by Chris Fowler, through Kim claims the approved spelling. The key figures in this bowel movement are, sadly, Nicholas Royle, Mark Morris, Joel Lane, Conrad Williams, Chris Kenworthy and myself. The defining features of Miserablist texts were that they be weird short stories, written by middle-class English men in their middle twenties, using the supernatural or unusual to whine about the world, their friends, and how their partner (or ex-partner) is doing them wrong. And that life is just depressing and horrible and nobody understands how ticked off about it all we are. And that we haven't got a nice girlfriend at the moment, and we'd really, really like one.

"There are threads of Miserablism in many of my early stories, but **Foreign Bodies** represents the zenith (or nadir) of the movement's influence in my work. I got a lot of things out my system for once and for all. I've done this stuff now, and I thank everyone for their patience. I still think it is, however, quite a good story."

B16a - Lethal Kisses - United Kingdom: Orion 1996. Edited by Ellen Datlow.
    B16a.1 - Hardcover priced at £15.99, ISBN: 1857984803.
    B16a.2 - Trade paperback priced at £9.99, ISBN: 1857984811.

B16b - Lethal Kisses - United Kingdom: Orion 1997 - mass market paperback priced at £5.99, ISBN: 0752808478. Edited by Ellen Datlow.

B16c - Appeared in **A5**.

B17 SORTED

"Nicholas Royle did more than anybody to encourage my writing in the very beginning. A couple of years ago he was putting together a Football-related anthology called **A Game of Two Halves**, and suggested I submit a story. I know absolutely nothing about soccer, as he knows, and have failed to be seduced by the fin-de-siecle 'Football's great, really it is, it's not just a bunch of overpaid louts booting a ball around, it's really post-modern and cool' school of thought.

"So I wrote **Sorted**. It's not a very nice story. Sorry."

B17a - A Book of Two Halves: New Football Short Stories - United Kingdom: Gollancz 1996 - trade paperback priced at £9.99, ISBN: 0575063238. Edited by Nicholas Royle.

B17b - A Book of Two Halves - United Kingdom: Indigo 1996 - mass market paperback priced at £5.99, ISBN: 0575400978. Edited by Nicholas Royle.

B17c - Appeared in **A5**.

B17d - as "Sistemato!" - in "Fuori Area" - Italy: Mondadori 2000 - paperback priced at L15,000.00, ISBN: 8804464283. Translated by Lea Maria Iandiori. Edited by Nicholas Royle.

B18 SOMEONE ELSE'S PROBLEM

"A story inspired by a train journey from London to Cambridge, to visit a then-girlfriend. It was the sight of a very small hand-print on the window which kicked it all off. That's the nicest way for stories to come, in many ways, and it's why I'd always rather make long journeys in England by train, rather than by car. There's something quite dreamlike about the rail experience (and I don't mean the nightmarish quality of the food). The slow pull out of the station, with its edificial architecture, huge pillars and vaulted ceilings; the tromp across the countryside, always seeing the back of things, the undersigned and unregarded backstage areas of life; and finally the approach into another town, another large and soot-stained portal. It's time out of time, and beats sitting in traffic any day."

B18a - Chills - United Kingdom: British Fantasy Society 1996 - magazine priced at £3.00, issue number #10. Edited by Peter Coleborn.

B19   HELL HATH ENLARGED HERSELF

"Both this story and **A Long Walk, For The Last Time** came about, indirectly, from a conversation I once had with a medium. She wasn't a professional, complete with crystal ball and vague talk of the beyond, merely someone who appeared to have an 'ability'. I'd never been a great believer in this sort of thing, but something about this woman - her matter of factness, along a kind of odd quality which she seemed to exude - made me take it a little more seriously after that. I had long nurtured a desire for some kind of paranormal ability, not least because it would be proof of what I dearly believe - that there is some weird and groovy stuff out there, just beyond what we normally see. But what, I thought, if you had this ability - and instead of being able to communicate with the living's loved ones, you could only receive messages from the people who'd hurt them most?

"The only other mildly interesting thing about this story is that it was the first time in my fiction that I used locations in which I had grown up. My family did indeed live in Gainesville when I was a child, and Crescent Beach and Sarasota were perennial holiday destinations."

B19a - Dark Terrors 2: The Gollancz Book of Horror - United Kingdom: Gollancz 1996 - hardcover priced at £16.99, ISBN: 0575063262. Edited by Stephen Jones and David Sutton.

B19aa - Proof copy in wraps.

B19b - Dark Terrors 2 - United Kingdom: Vista 1997 - mass market paperback priced at £5.99, ISBN: 057560235X. Edited by Stephen Jones and David Sutton.

B19c - The Mammoth Book of Best New Horror 8 - United Kingdom: Robinson 1997 - trade paperback priced at £6.99, ISBN: 1854879014. Edited by Stephen Jones.

B19d - The Mammoth Book of Best New Horror 8 - United States: Carroll & Graf 1997 - trade paperback priced at $10.95, ISBN: 0786704748. Edited by Stephen Jones.

B19e - Appeared in **A5**.

B19f - as "Die Banner Der Hölle" - in "Psycho-Express" - Germany: Blitz/Edition Metzengerstein 2000 - unpriced, ISBN: 3932171233. Anthology edited by Frank Festa.

B19g - Appeared in **A9**.

B20 NOT WAVING

"As will probably not be a surprise to anyone who's read my fiction, especially the novels, I'm a big fan of cats. For many years, while I was batting around London in a number of short-term lets, none of them on the ground floor (I don't like ground floor flats; they feel smaller and I don't give a monkey's about having access to a garden, south-facing or otherwise) I was unable to have a cat of my own. Instead I had virtual cats, like the one in this story. Now that I'm more settled, we have two very beautiful cats - Spangle and Lintilla - both of whom are currently asleep on my lap. They have done this for a large proportion of each day since they were very little kittens. They are now significantly larger, which means I have to work in a half-lotus position. This may be more information than you need."

B20a - Twists of the Tale - United States: Dell 1996 - mass market paperback priced at $5.50, ISBN: 0440217717. Edited by Ellen Datlow.

B20b - The Year's Best Fantasy and Horror: Tenth Annual Collection - United States: St. Martin's Press 1997. Edited by Ellen Datlow and Terri Windling.

B20b1- Hardcover priced at $29.95, ISBN: 0312157002.
B20b2 - Trade paperback priced at $17.95, ISBN: 0312157010.

B20c - as "Sans un adieu" - in "Contes du chat pervers" - France: J'ai Lu 1999 - paperback, unpriced, ISBN: 2290053473. Edited by Ellen Datlow.

B20d - as "Der mann, der katzen leid zufügte" - in "Das grobe lesebuch der fantastischen katzengeschicter" - Germany: Blauvalt Verlag 2001 - paperback priced at DM15.00, ISBN: 3442249635. Translated by Joachim Körber. Edited by Ellen Datlow.

B20e - Appeared in **A9**.

B21 SAVE AS...

"Computers have brought a lot of groovy things into our lives, notably being able to edit what you've written without retyping the sodding thing, and spend afternoons blowing the crap out of seven types of gun-wielding polygon-based alien psychopaths. It struck me that there are more fundamental elements of the way they work that would be really nice in real life: like having a Search function, so you could rapidly find the book or car keys or spare pack of stale cigarettes which you know have to be in the house somewhere; or being able to back up when things are going well.

"But, of course, computers are at least as fallible as anything else in life. Often, more so."

B21a - Interzone - United Kingdom: Interzone 1997 - magazine priced at £2.75, number #115 (January). Edited by David Pringle.

B21b - Appeared in **A3**.

B21c - Appeared in **A5**.

B21d - as "Speichern unter..." - in "Von kommenden Schrecken" (Of Coming

Horrors) - Germany: FKSFL (Freundeskreis Science Fiction Leipzig) 2000 - hardcover, unpriced, no ISBN. An anthology produced for Elstercon 2000 in Leipzig, Germany. Edited by Dirk Berger, Thomas Braatz, Mario Franke, Manfred Orlowski and Frank Ruschel. Cover art by Mario Franke.

B21e - As "Sauvegarde" - in Galaxies - France: June 2003 - magazine priced at €10.00, ISBN: 2951972415. Issue 29.

B21f - Appeared in **A9**.

B22 CHARMS

"I wrote this story initially to send to a couple of lovely gentlemen who were celebrating the culture of the pop single*. Not surprisingly - as it's not even slightly about singles - they rejected it. In the end, years later, it was published first by **AbeSea** *magazine and then in Peter Crowther's* **Taps and Sighs***, which was the ideal home for it. I'd never really known exactly what I was getting at in the story until - after this second publishing - Stephen Jones said: 'It's a ghost story, where the ghost is a year'. Actually he's right."*

B22a - AbeSea - United Kingdom 1997. Broadsheet magazine priced at £2.00, undated, issue J.

B22b - Taps and Sighs - United States: Subterranean Press 2000. Released in three limited states. Edited by Peter Crowther, cover art by J.K. Potter.
- **B22b.1** - Limited trade edition - hardcover priced at $35.00, ISBN: 189228474X.
- **B22b.2** - Limited edition - 500 numbered hardcover copies priced at $50.00, ISBN: 1892284375. Signed by all contributors.
- **B22b.3** - Lettered edition - 52 lettered slipcased hardcover copies priced at $195.00, ISBN: 1892284499. Signed by all contributors. Additionally signed by J.K. Potter, Richard Matheson and Douglas Winter.

B22c - Appeared in **A9**.

---

*Kim Newman and Paul J. McAuley's **In Dreams**, published in paperback by Gollancz in 1992. A rather scarce paperback, it includes early stories by Peter Hamilton, Alastair Reynolds and Stephen Baxter, to name but three.

michael marshall smith
an annotated bibliography

B23 DEAR ALISON

"Many of the stories I have written have been set in or very near places I lived. For a number of years I hopped around North London, spending about nine months at a time in a variety of different apartments. This story, with its walk down from Kentish Town to the centre of London, passes several of them."

B23a - The Mammoth Book of Dracula: Vampire Tales for the New Millennium - United Kingdom: Robinson 1997 - trade paperback priced at £6.99, ISBN: 1854875205. Edited by Stephen Jones.

B23b - The Mammoth Book of Dracula: Vampire Tales for the New Millennium - United States: Carroll & Graf 1997 - trade paperback priced at $10.95, ISBN: 0786704284. Edited by Stephen Jones.

B23c - as "Cara Alison" - in "Il Grande Libro di Dracula" - Italy: Newton & Compton 2000 - trade paperback priced at L22900.00, ISBN: 8882893286. Edited by Stephen Jones.

B23d - Keep Out the Night - United Kingdom: PS Publishing 2002. Edited by Stephen Jones. The story appears in a revised version.
    B23d.1 - 500 hardcover copies priced at £45.00/$65.00, ISBN: 1902880544. Signed by Stephen Jones.
    B23d.2 - 100 hardcover copies priced at £65.00/$90.00, ISBN: 1902880552. Signed by all contributors.

B23e - Appeared in **A9**.

B24 VICTORIA'S SECRET

*"This story, like **The Dark Land** and many others, took its initial impulse from a dream. Not mine, in this case: simply one I was told and then appropriated for my own dastardly ends."*

B24a - Dark of the Night - United Kingdom: Pumpkin Books 1997. Released in two states. Edited by Stephen Jones. Illustrations by Randy Broecker.

> **B24a.1** - Trade edition - hardcover priced at £15.99, ISBN: 1901914011.
> **B24a.2** - Limited edition - 250 numbered slipcased hardcover copies priced at £25.00, ISBN: 1901914003. Signed by all contributors.

B25 DIFFERENT NOW

"An early story, set near the first flat I had in London - in Finsbury Park. This story shows quite a Ramsey Campbell influence, I suspect. I like it because it reminds me of that time, when I'd just started writing, and was living and working in London for the first time. Though, as the story suggests, not everything was tickety boo..."

B25a - Scaremongers - United Kingdom: Tanjen 1997 - paperback priced at £6.99, ISBN: 1901530078. Edited by Andrew Haigh.

B26 WALKING WOUNDED

"The genesis of this story came in two parts. The basic idea, of the returning wounds, was a very old one that I never quite came up with a forum for. Then, after moving from a very lovely flat to a not very lovely one (as outlined in the story) I came up with the rest of it. Quite a lot of the story is true, including the breaking of two ribs during the move. It was hell."

B26a - Dark Terrors 3: The Gollancz Book of Horror - United Kingdom: Gollancz

1997 - hardcover priced at £16.99, ISBN: 0575065168. Edited by Stephen Jones and David Sutton.
   B26aa - Proof copy in wraps.

B26b - Dark Terrors 3 - United Kingdom: Vista 1998 - mass market paperback priced at £6.99, ISBN: 0575603984. Edited by Stephen Jones and David Sutton.

B27 MR. CAT

"This isn't really a story, but a short memoir of a couple of events surrounding the cat my family used to have, written for an anthology of supernatural experiences."

B27a - Dancing With The Dark: True Encounters with the Paranormal by Masters of the Macabre - United Kingdom: Vista 1997 - mass market paperback priced at £5.99, ISBN: 0575601663. Edited by Stephen Jones.
   B27aa - Proof copy in wraps.

B27b - "Valcik S Temnotou" - Czechoslovakia: Apsida-Knizni Klub 1998 - hardcover, ISBN: 8090230393. Edited by Stephen Jones.

B27c - Dancing With The Dark: True Encounters with the Paranormal by Masters of the Macabre - United States: Carroll & Graf 1999 - trade paperback priced at $12.95, ISBN: 0786706201. Edited by Stephen Jones.

B27d - "La Danza delle Tenebre" - Italy: Bompiani 1999 - trade paperback priced at L14500.00, ISBN: 8845241181. Edited by Stephen Jones.

B28 MISSED CONNECTION

"Like many stories, this one initially came about from something that actually happened. I went into central London one day on the Underground. I had an appalling head cold, and got awfully confused about different sides of tube carriages. I just couldn't work it out. Eventually, of course, my head cleared - but the question always remains: 'What if you weren't confused? What if you were right?'"

B28a - Secret City: Strange Tales of London - United Kingdom: World Fantasy Convention in association with Titan Books 1997. Released in two states. Edited by Stephen Jones and Jo Fletcher, cover art by Bob Egleton. The book of the 1997 London World Fantasy Convention.

    B28a.1 - Trade edition - oversized trade paperback, unpriced, ISBN: 1852869496.

    B28a.2 - Limited edition - hardcover limited to 300 numbered copies, unpriced, ISBN: 1852869488.

B29 EVERYBODY GOES

"The block of flats referred to in this story is loosely based on a place where my family lived in Armidale, in New South Wales, Australia. One day we went out to visit the family of a school chum of mine, who lived in the outback. While the parents chatted and did grown-up things, my friend took me out into the bush and showed me some things he knew. It was a hot day, and the land was flat and featureless. We found this little canyon in the middle of the open plain, much as described in the story, with steep walls and a door floating in the pond at the bottom.

"In retrospect I suppose that if someone had taken the trouble to drag a piece of rubbish that heavy to it then we can't have been that far from civilisation - but in my memory we were on the surface of Mars. We messed around, as boys will, and we had fun, and then we walked home through the stillness. It was a good day."

B29a - Appeared in **A3**.

B29b - Appeared in **A5**.

B29c - The Third Alternative - United Kingdom: TTA Press 1999 - magazine priced at £3.75, issue 19. Edited by Andy Cox.

B29d - The Mammoth Book of Best New Horror 10 - United Kingdom: Robinson 1999 - trade paperback priced at £6.99, ISBN: 1841190640. Edited by Stephen Jones.

B29e - The Mammoth Book of Best New Horror 10 - United States: Caroll & Graf 1999 - trade paperback priced at $10.95, ISBN: 0786706902. Edited by Stephen Jones.

B29f - As "Basof Kulam Holchim" - United Kingdom: privately published 2000. Released in two limited states. Translated into Hebrew with introduction by Lavie Tidhar. Cover and two internal illustrations by Joseph Locker. Signed by LT, JL and MMS*.
> **B29f.1** - Lettered edition - 22 lettered (in Hebrew) staple-bound copies in yellow card covers, unpriced, no ISBN.
> **B29f.2** - PC edition - 10 staple-bound copies in green card covers, marked PC, unpriced, no ISBN.

B29g - Appeared in **A9**.

B30 WHEN GOD LIVED IN KENTISH TOWN

> "I shouldn't be too harsh about corporate videos, because they paid my rent for a long time when short stories sure as hell weren't doing so. On the other hand, they are surely amongst the lowest forms of human endeavour. I actually met some rather nice people while writing them, which somehow makes it worse: I hate the idea of all those talented and dedicated individuals giving themselves (and their scriptwriters) ulcers, all to produce fifteen minutes of bollocks.
> "When I wrote this story I had just come off the back of writing six videos on the trot about floor-cleaning apparatuses (this was for a company other than Hoover, so of course I couldn't call them that in the script, though everyone else in the world does) and 'white goods'. Fridges, in other words. And washing machines. And freezers, and tumble driers. Christ it was dull. It was dull with big wheels and a flashing light.

*One set of A4 printer proofs produced.

"Hour after hour of meetings and corporate claptrap set the scene for this story, along with the fact that there really did use to be an odd little electrical store in Kentish Town, more or less where it's described. I went in there one day, out of curiosity, and bought a broken watch.

"Not sure why."

B30a - Appeared in **A3**.

B30b - Appeared in **A5**.

B30c - Appeared in **A9**.

B31 A CONVENIENT ARRANGEMENT

"The strange thing about bibliographies, as I've implied elsewhere, is that things come out of order. This story is a very short and early one, and yet appeared much later - only when someone happened to be doing a very big anthology of very short stories."

B31a - Horrors! 365 Scary Stories: Get Your Daily Dose of Terror - United States: Barnes and Noble 1998 - hardcover priced at $12.98, ISBN: 0760701415. Edited by Dziemianowicz, Weinberg and Greenberg.

B31b - Cemetery Dance - United States: Cemetery Dance Publications 1999 - magazine priced at $4.00, Issue 31. Edited by Richard Chizmar.

michael marshall smith
an annotated bibliography

B32 A PLACE TO STAY

"This story grew out of a visit to New Orleans for the World Fantasy Convention. Very little of what is described actually happened, apart from the hangovers, though I can heartily recommend the muffellettas in the French Bar. And Jimmy Buffet's, too. By co-incidence, it was while getting drunk in the Jimmy Buffet's in Key West that I had some of the initial ideas for my novella **The Vaccinator**, *which also features a reference to one of his bars. I should obviously get drunk in Jimmy Buffet's more often. And maybe receive a fee for the product placement."*

B32a - Dark Terrors 4: The Gollancz Book of Horror - United Kingdom: Gollancz 1998 - hardcover priced at £16.99, ISBN: 0575065818. Edited by Stephen Jones and David Sutton.
    B32aa - Proof copy in wraps.

B32b - Dark Terrors 4 - United Kingdom: Millennium 1999 - mass market paperback priced at £6.99, ISBN: 1857988949.

B32c - Appeared in **A5**.

B32d - The Year's Best Fantasy and Horror: Twelfth Annual Collection - United States: St. Martin's Press 1999. Edited by Ellen Datlow and Terri Windling.
    B32d.1 - Hardcover priced at $29.95, ISBN: 0312209622.
    B32d.2 - Trade paperback priced at $17.95, ISBN: 0312206860.

B32e - Appeared in **A9**.

B33 ENOUGH PIZZA

"There's not much to say about this story except that it's not based on anyone in particular, and that I think it's the only story I've ever written which has not a whisper of the supernatural or science fictional or horrific about it. Also, don't ever go to the hotel mentioned. It's shite."

B33a - The Ex Files: New Stories about Old Flames - United Kingdom: Quartet 1998 - trade paperback priced at £7.00, ISBN: 0704380803. Edited by Nicholas Royle.

60

B33b - Appeared in **A9**.

B34 DIET HELL

"Don't you just hate putting on weight? And wouldn't you rather do just about anything to take it off again, except, of course, actually eating and drinking less and doing some exercise? Those are too hard. There must be some other way. There must. I demand it."

B34a - Appeared in **A3**.

B34b - Appeared in **A5**.

B35 THE GAP

*"I've referred to a few other stories by saying they were overly early ones and this is another of those. By that I mean that they were one of a group of about five or six stories I wrote after I did **The Man Who Drew Cats**. That first story had kind of thrown me into the idea of writing, and was actually quite long. The next few were much shorter, and quite different from one another, almost as if I was trying to confirm the kind of thing I was going to be writing about. **The Gap** came about from me noticing a motorbike abandoned on a motorway, much as described in the story. It also features a notion I'd been playing with, that of un-observed environments. It was never published in its own right, but found a place in the Special Edition of **Spares**, because the gap mentioned was one of the inspirations for the more developed realm of the same name in that novel."*

B35a - appeared in **A2u**.

B36 WELCOME

*"This is a very early story, though it didn't get printed for some years. When this happens, only rarely is it a case of the writer grubbing around in the 'not sold yet' file in order to fulfil a request: it is far more usually the case that the story simply took that long to settle down. Often I've written things quickly, sold them quickly, and that's that. There are a few others which I've tinkered with over the years, gradually honing it down, changing the emphasis here and there, until it's ready to leave the hard disk. **Welcome**, which was first written in 1989 and only published in 1999, is my most extreme example of this. It was inspired by two things: the rather crap life I had at the time, and the fact that the event*

referred to near the beginning - an erroneous date on a file - actually happened."

B36a - White Of The Moon - United Kingdom: Pumpkin 1999 - hardcover limited to 1000 copies, priced at £16.99, ISBN: 1901914135. Edited by Stephen Jones.

B36b - Mammoth Book of Best New Horror 11 - United Kingdom: Robinson 2000 - trade paperback priced at £6.99, ISBN: 1841191671. Edited by Stephen Jones.

B36c - Mammoth Book of Best New Horror 11 - United States: Carroll & Graf 2000 - trade paperback priced at $11.95, ISBN: 0786707925. Edited by Stephen Jones.

B36d - The Year's Best Fantasy and Horror, Thirteenth Annual Collection - United States: St. Martin's Press 2000. Edited by Ellen Datlow and Terry Windling.
    B36d.1 - Hardcover priced at $29.95, ISBN: 0312262744.
    B36d.2 - Trade paperback priced at $17.95, ISBN: 031226416X.

B37 THE BOOK OF IRRATIONAL NUMBERS

"Something always happens when I'm supposed to be writing a novel. I suddenly get very, very interested in something other than the subject of the novel. At various times this has included learning Egyptian hieroglyphs, playing the banjo, and mathematics. I genuinely thought there might actually be a book in the maths thing, but it hasn't happened yet. In the meantime at least I got a story out of it. And it was a lot less hard on the ears than me learning the banjo, at which I was utterly crap."

B37a - 999 - United States: Hill House and Cemetery Dance 1999. Released in two limited states. Edited by Al Sarrantonio.

    B37a.1 - Numbered edition - 500 slipcased hardcover copies bound in black leather, priced at $125.00, ISBN: 18811475972. Signed by all contributors except Stephen King and Joyce Carol Oates.

B27a.2 - Lettered edition - 52 slipcased hardcover copies bound in red leather, priced at $350.00, same ISBN as **B37a.1**.

B37b - 999 - United States: Avon 1999 - hardcover priced at $27.50, ISBN 0380997400.
    B37bb - Proof copy in illustrated wraps.

B37c - 999 - United Kingdom: Hodder & Stoughton 1999.
    B37c.1 - Hardcover priced at £17.99, ISBN 0340748591.
    B37c.2 - Trade paperback priced at £9.99, ISBN 0340748613.

B37d - 999 - Germany: Wilhelm Heyne Verlag 1999 - hardcover priced at DM33.00, ISBN: 345316567.

B37e - 999 - France: Le Grande Livre Du Mois 1999 - hardcover, unpriced, ISBN: 2702839908 . Possibly a book club edition.

B37f - 999 - France: Albin Michel 1999 - trade paperback priced at FF160.00, ISBN: 222610747.

B37g - 666 - Italy: Edizione Mondolibri 1999 - hardcover, second of two volumes, the first being "999". Book club edition.

B37h - 999 - Japan: Tokyo Sogensha 1999 - trade paperback priced at ¥780.00, ISBN: 4488584020. Second of three volumes.

B37i - 999 - United Kingdom: Hodder & Stoughton 2000 - mass market paperback priced at £7.99 ISBN: 0340748605.

B37j - 666 - Italy: Sterling & Kupfer 2000 - hardcover priced at L32900.00, ISBN: 8820030047. Second of two volumes, the first being "999".

B37k - 999 - France: Albin Michel 2000 - paperback priced at FF55.00, ISBN: 2253149926.

B37l - 999 - Germany: Wilhelm Heyne Verlag 2001 - paperback priced at DM20.00, ISBN: 3453177533.

B37m - Appeared in **A9**.

B38 THE HANDOVER

"An idea I had during a fantastic month-long drive across the USA. Popped pretty full-grown into my head, but for some reason I waited a year or two before writing it. Sometimes it's like that. You know what you're going to do, but it just isn't quite time to do it.

"Oh yes - 'laziness': that's what it's called."

B38a - Dark Terrors 5: The Gollancz Book of Horror - United Kingdom: Gollancz 2000. Edited by Stephen Jones and David Sutton.
    B38a.1 - Hardcover priced at £17.99, ISBN: 057507048X.
    B38a.2 - Trade paperback priced at £12.99, ISBN: 0575070498.

B38b - Dark Terrors 5 - United Kingdom: Gollancz 2001 - paperback priced at £6.99, ISBN: 185798322X. Edited by Stephen Jones and David Sutton.

B38c - The Mammoth Book of Best New Horror 12 - United Kingdom: Robinson 2001 - mass market paperback priced at £6.99 ISBN: 1841192929. Edited by Stephen Jones.

B38d - The Mammoth Book of Best New Horror 12 - United States: Carroll & Graf 2001 - trade paperback priced at $11.95, ISBN 0786709197. Edited by Stephen Jones.

B38e - Appeared in **A9**.

B39 WHAT YOU MAKE IT

"This is a result of visiting Disney World and Key West in the same vacation, and reading some Hemingway on the journey. It's also about how I feel about the world. The magic's there: use it or lose it. Lot of people don't like Disney World. I do. I think it's fabulous."

B39a - Appeared in **A5**.

B39b - Appeared in **B36d**.

B39c - Appeared in **A9**.

B40 SOME WITCH'S BED

"Not really a story, this is a short vignette inspired by the Belly song 'Witches'. Like all good songs, it seems to evoke a hell of a lot more than the few words in it seem capable of - and in this case, while listening to it for the first time many years ago, it seemed to conjure up a whole Bradbury-esque world. This short piece was written for an anthology about October, which seemed to suit it."

B40a - October Dreams - United States: Cemetery Dance 2001. Released in three states. Edited by Richard Chizmar and Robert Morrish.
    B40a.1 - Trade edtion - hardcover priced at $40.00, ISBN: 1587670119.
    B40a.2 - Numbered edition - 450 slipcased hardcover copies bound in leather, same ISBN as **B40a.1**. Signed by all contributors.
    B40a.3 - Lettered edition - 52 traycased hardcover copies, same ISBN as **B40a.1**. Signed by all contributors.

B40b - October Dreams - United States: Roc 2002 - trade paperback priced at $16.00, ISBN: 0451458958. Edited by Richard Chizmar and Robert Morrish.

B41 LAST GLANCE BACK

*"It doesn't happen very often now - because short story writing all too often gets squeezed out by other commitments - but there have been a few times when I've written a short story, thought 'Well, I've no idea who'd buy that', and stuck it in a folder for later. That was the case with this one, with the added - but again, not unknown - feature that I wasn't sure I'd nailed it, but couldn't see why. I took it out every now and then and worked on it, getting it closer to something I could be happy with, and then finally in 2001 was happy to place it in **GIRLS' NIGHT OUT / BOYS' NIGHT IN**. I didn't get paid (it was a book for charity), but at least it found a home, and by then had been cajoled into shape."*

B41a - Girls' Night Out/Boys' Night In - United Kingdom: HarperCollins 2001 - paperback priced at £6.99, ISBN: 0007122039. Edited by Chris Manby, Fiona Walker and Jessica Adams.
    B41aa - proof copy in illustrated wraps.

B41b - Girls Night In/Gentlemen by Invitation - Australia: Penguin Books 2002 - paperback, unpriced, ISBN 0143000047.

B41c - Appeared in **A9**.

B42 THEY ALSO SERVE

"I had the idea for this story a long, long time ago, and just didn't do anything with it. I knew enough at the time to worry that it was perhaps kind of a traditional - in the sense of 'old-fashioned' - science fiction kind of story, and that it wouldn't sit well in a genre which was then very taken with cyberspace and nanobots.

"But then, when I agreed to do a little book of my cat stories for Paul Miller and Earthling Publications, I remembered the idea and thought fuck it: I don't care if it's old-fashioned. Fashion is just fashion, and old-fashioned sometimes works. I hope it does here."

B42a Appeared in **A7**.

B42b - Appeared in **A9**.

B43 TWO SHOT

*"This was another of those ideas which had been in the back of my mind for quite a while, waiting for the impetus to actually start it. This finally came in the form of a request from Al Sarrantonio for a story for his **Redshift** collection and - as is often the way - once the story was begun it came out very quickly. As Al notes in his introductory piece in the book, it became easily the fastest acceptance I've ever had: he happened to be online when I emailed it; he read it immediately and sent back a 'yes', which I picked up very soon afterwards. A pleasingly quasi-futuristic process for one of my rare sf short stories..."*

B43a - Redshift: Extreme Visions of Speculative Fiction - United States: Roc 2001 - hardcover priced at $24.95, ISBN: 0451458591. Edited by Al Sarrantonio.

B43b - Redshift: Extreme Visions of Speculative Fiction - United States: Roc 2002 - paperback priced at $7.99, ISBN: 0451459040. Edited by Al Sarrantonio.

B43c - Appeared in **A9**.

B44 NIGHT FALLS, AGAIN

"This story, published in a collection honouring the bizarre visual concoctions of JK Potter, went through an unusual creative process.

"I had been recently asked to provide a story both for this anthology and for another, by an entirely different publisher. The way in which the JK Potter anthology worked was that all the invited contributors were sent a set of Potter's images, and asked to choose one on which to base a story. I did so - selecting a powerful picture of a man whose head metamorphosed at the back into that of an alligator - and then put the job to one side to concentrate on something else. In the meantime, Brett Savoury invited me to contribute to an anthology he was putting together based around the idea of chiaroscuro, the interplay of light and shade.

"What happened then was that I wrote the same story for both anthologies, despite their having entirely different remits, and they both accepted it, but only one published it.

"I wrote a chiaroscuro story for Brett, but was aware while doing so that I was also being heavily influenced by Potter's very striking image - not least because it was sitting on my desk, propped up against the computer. There were times, in fact, where I had to steer myself away from ideas - and cut a few lines here and there - because they were more appropriate to the Potter image than the chiaroscuro concept. My head was thinking about light and shade, but my heart was stuck on the image. Slightly confused by this, I sent the end result to Brett, who accepted it.

"'Hmm,' I thought. Now I need to write a story about that picture, but... part of me already thinks I've done it.

"I was still musing ineffectively about what to do about this, when sad news came in from Brett: the publishing deal for the chiaroscuro anthology had folded. So I took the story back, re-instated some stuff that had been in the first draft, rewrote a little, this time just holding the Potter image in my head, and sent it to Bill Schafer at Subterranean - explaining what had happened.

"Happily, he accepted the story too."

B44a - Embrace The Mutation: Fiction Inspired by the Art of J.K. Potter - United States: Subterranean Press 2002. Released in three states. Edited by William Schafer and Bill Sheehan, cover and other artwork by J.K. Potter.
    B44a.1 - Trade edition - hardcover priced at $40.00.
    B44a.2 - Numbered edition - 500 hardcover copies priced at $100.00. Signed by all contributors.
    B44a.3 - Lettered edition - 26 traycased hardcover copies priced at $500.00. Signed by all contributors.

B45 A LONG WALK, FOR THE LAST TIME

"As noted more fully earlier (see **Hell Hath Enlarged Herself***), I once met someone who might have been a medium, and the conversation indirectly led to ideas for two stories. I've always rather liked it as a story, but it took a while to find the right place to publish it. It's funny the way that works. Some stories bounce straight from your head to the page and then ricochet straight out into a collection. Others wander only very slowly from one state to the next, sometimes settling down for years along the way. These latter stories end up feeling like a part of your life, and it's often hard to make an objective decision as to whether they're any good."*

B45a - Dark Terrors 6: The Gollancz Book of Horror - United Kingdom: Gollancz 2002. Edited by Stephen Jones and David Sutton.
    B45a.1 - Hardcover priced at £17.99, ISBN: 0575072482.
    B45a.2 - Trade paperback priced at £9.99, ISBN: 0575072490.

B45b - Appeared in **A9**.

B46 BEING RIGHT

"I've written a lot of stories about being single, or about having a girlfriend. I think 'Being Right' is the first about being married, which means it's only taken my imagination five years to catch up with reality.

"Now, you shouldn't take away from this the idea that the story in any way accurately represents my own marriage; just the kind of directions in which relationships can develop, over the longer term. So much of popular culture is dedicated to celebrating the moment of falling in love, or the morning after, or the day you get married (in this lovey-dovey fictional universe, it's always about six months later, and it never rains, unless it can do so with heart-warming comic

potential). After that, the lovers become mere 'parents' ('Jimmy - you're grounded!'), or slide into the role of 'couple gone bad, soon to be unleashed back into the great story as two divorcees' (cue 'Sleepless in Seattle' music).

"But actually, real stuff happens to married people. Not just affairs, breaking up, childbirth. Real, mundane, stuff.

"I don't have any particular views on the sanctity of marriage or otherwise, but it's a pretty cool state of affairs to be in. You should try it. No, not you, I meant those other people."

B46a - Appeared in **A9**.

B47 MAYBE NEXT TIME

"I gave this to Nicholas Royle to read - he reads most of my stuff soon after completion, as does the writer Conrad Williams, and my wife - and he told me it was a melancholy story about feeling one was getting old.

"I think he's right. The main character has his fortieth birthday during the course of the story, and mine is only a few years away now. I have no idea how this state of affairs came about. Time passes, I guess.

"Though I am still, of course, a young buck inside.

"Everybody is."

B47a - Appeared in **A9**.

B48 THE MUNCHIES

"I wrote this story a long time ago, sat on it for a while, tinkered with it, and then gave to a magazine who'd made a request (I wasn't getting many requests back then). The magazine in question then took a long, slow, leisurely time in disappearing off the face of the earth, and it was a good few years before I realised that **The Munchies** was back on the market. By that time it sat a little oddly with the kind of stuff I was usually doing, and I didn't look too hard to find a home for it - though I did read it occasionally, for fun. Then when we were putting together the Earthling anthology I looked at it again and thought 'Actually, that's okay'.

"It's about being stoned.

"It is not based on a true story, though it does very strongly bring back a certain period in my life."

B48a - Appeared in **A9**.

B49 OPEN DOORS

"I have a terrible tendency to see grass as being greener - or at least more interesting - on the other side of fences. All fences. When I see those 'Real Footage Of People Falling On Their Ass!' shows on television, I spend most of the time looking at the backgrounds, wondering where that door goes, or what's the other side of that hill, or what his family or her cooking is like. It's not that I'm not happy with my own life, it's just that all the other stuff, all the other lives (however stone-cold-dull they may be in reality) has such a mesmerising lure, through being different and unknown. Just different. I guess it's similar to the fact that food always tastes better when made by someone else; the other, the outside, stuff that's fresh - it's fascinating.

"I also suppose that feeling like this is part of what compels one to be a writer. Anyway. **Open Doors** is a story about a man who takes this to extremes. It's an idea I'd had for quite a while, but then one day - much as with the narrator - I happened to be going for a walk and saw a way into it."

B49a - Appeared in **A9**.

B50 THE RIGHT MEN

"This was one of those cases where I'd had the basic idea for quite a long time, but hadn't found a sufficiently compelling way of enticing it out of my head and onto the page. Then I happened to be at a literary festival in the South of France where I met Colin Wilson, a long-time inspiration. In the course of a few wine-fuelled discussions we touched upon the idea of a certain type of man who has the ability to make others do what he wants through pure alpha-maledom (we were talking about it in the context of cult leaders). When I got home I realised the story was ready to go. The idea was there already, of course, but after talking about it, it just seemed more straightforward. Once I'd got that sorted, the story came out in a day."

B50a - Gathering the Bones - Australia: HarperCollins 2003 - trade paperback priced at AUS$29.95, ISBN: 0732270243. Edited by Jack Dann, Ramsey Campbell and Dennis Etchison.

B50b - Gathering the Bones - United States: Tor 2003 - hardcover priced at $27.95, ISBN: 0765301784. Edited by Jack Dann, Ramsey Campbell and Dennis Etchison.

B50c - Gathering the Bones - United States: Tor 2003 - trade paperback priced at $15.95, ISBN: 0765301792. Edited by Jack Dann, Ramsey Campbell and Dennis Etchison.

michael marshall smith
an annotated bibliography

Non-English Editions

Polish - One of Us

Japanese - Spares

German - One of Us

French - One of Us

Polish - Spares

German - Spares

72

Non-English Editions

Italian - One of Us

Greek - Spares

Hebrew - Spares

Portugese - Spares

Japanese - Only Forward

German - Only Forward

73

michael marshall smith
an annotated bibliography

C Selected Non-Fiction

C1 READ THIS

C1a - Appeared in "The New York Review of Science Fiction" - United States: Dragon Press 1995 - magazine priced at $3.50, number 79 (March), volume 7, number 7.

C2 INTRODUCTION

C2a - Appeared in "The Longest Single Note And Other Strange Compositions" - United States: Cemetery Dance Publications 1999. A collection of writings by Peter Crowther. Released in two states. Cover art by Alan M. Clark.
- **C2aa** - Proof copy in illustrated wraps.
- **C2a.1** - Numbered edition - 500 numbered hardcover copies priced at $40.00, ISBN: 1881475565. Signed by PC and MMS.
- **C2a.2** - Lettered edition - 26 slipcased hardcover copies. Signed by all contributors

C3 INTRODUCTION

C3a - Appeared in "Waltzes and Whispers" - United Kingdom: Pumpkin Books 1999. A collection of short stories by Jay Russell. Hardcover priced at £16.99, ISBN: 190191416X. Limited to 750 copies.*

C4 WHAT IF?

C4a - Appeared in "T3" - United Kingdom: Future Publishing 1998 - magazine, issue 25 (October).

C5 UNTITLED

C5a - Appeared in "Poddities: A Creative Tribute to Jack Finney's Novel The Body Snatchers" - United States: Day Off Publications 2000 - paperback priced at $8.00, no ISBN. Edited by Suzanne Donahue.

---

* An indeterminate number of copies with the same price and ISBN were bound up for library distribution with the dustjacket artwork printed directly on to the book's binding.

C6 UNTITLED

C6a - Appeared in "Dystopia" - United States: Gauntlet Press 2000. A collection of stories by Richard Matheson. Released in two states. Cover artwork by Harry Morris.
> **C6a.1** - Numbered edition - 500 hardcover copies signed by RM, HM and Peter Straub.
> **C6a.2** - Deluxe edition - 250 numbered hardcover copies signed by all contributors.

C7 UNTITLED

C7a - Appeared in "Tenebres" - France: Lueurs Mortes 2000/2001 - magazine priced at 130.00FF, number 11/12 (September 2000-January 2001). A double volume dedicated to Stephen King.

C8 INTRODUCTION

C8a - Appeared in "Nearly People" - United Kingdom: PS Publishing 2001. A novella by Conrad Williams. Cover art by Wieslaw Walkuski.
> **C8a.1** 300 numbered hardcover copies priced at £25.00, ISBN: 1902880196. Signed by CW and MMS.
> **C8a.2** 500 numbered paperback copies priced at £8.00, ISBN: 1902880188. Signed by CW.

C9 INTRODUCTION

C9a - "Lost In Space: Geographies of Science Fiction" - United Kingdom: Continuum 2002 - paperback priced at £16.99, ISBN: 0826457312. Edited by Rob Kitchin and James Kneale

C10 UNTITLED

C10a - Appeared in "What Walks Alone: A Creative Tribute to Shirley Jackson's The Haunting of Hill House" - United States: Succubus Press 2002 - paperback priced at $8.00. Edited by Suzanne Donahue.

D Selected Book Design

D1 CLIVE BARKER, MYTHMAKER FOR THE MILLENNIUM

D1a - "Clive Barker, Mythmaker for the Millennium" by Suzanna Barbieri - United Kingdom: British Fantasy Society 1994 - paperback priced at £4.99, ISBN: 0952415305. Introduction by Peter Atkins, cover art by Les Edwards, internal illustrations by Pete Queally.*

D2 QUETZALCON: THE KINGSTON DUNSTAN CONVENTION

D2a - "Quetzalcon: The Kingston Dunstan Convention" by Kim Newman - United Kingdom: Airgedlámh Publications 1997 - 800 staple-bound copies in card covers, unpriced, no ISBN. Spoof convention booklet/horror story. Signed by KN and MMS.

D3 SHADOWS OF LIGHT AND DARK

D3a - "Shadows Of Light and Dark" by Jo Fletcher - United Kingdom: Airgedlámh Publications/ The Alchemy Press 1998 - 250 hardcover copies priced at £12.99, ISBN: 09532261018. Introduction by Neil Gaiman, cover art by Les Edwards, author photograph by Seamus Ryan. Signed by all contributors.

D4 A SECRET HISTORY OF RANDY BROECKER

D4a - "A Secret History of Randy Broecker" - United Kingdom: Airgedlámh Publications, 2002 - 50 staple-bound numbered copies in card covers and envelope, unpriced, no ISBN. Illustrated by Randy Broecker. Chapbook to celebrate artist Broecker's 50th birthday party in London on January 22nd, 2002. Edited by Stephen Jones.

---

* While this is not a limited edition, approximately 75-100 copies were signed by Barker and Barbieri, though few by Smith.

D5 KEEP OUT THE NIGHT

D5a - see **B23d**.

D6 BY MOONLIGHT ONLY

D6a - By Moonlight Only - United Kingdom: PS Publishing 2003. Released in two states. Edited by Stephen Jones.
> **D6a.1** - 500 hardcover copies priced at £35.00, ISBN: 1902880714. Signed by Stephen Jones.
> **D6a.2** - 150 hardcover copies priced at £60.00, ISBN: 1902880722. Signed by all contributors.

E Selected Studies

E1 ALL-CONSUMING CRIMES OF CONSUMPTION: DETECTIVE FANTASIES IN THE NOVELS OF MICHAEL MARSHALL SMITH

E1a - "All-Consuming Crimes of Consumption: Detective Fantasies in the Novels of Michael Marshall Smith" by Matthew Hills.
> **E1a.1** - Appeared in "Foundation: The International Review of Science Fiction" - United Kingdom: The Science Fiction Foundation 2000 - a digest-sized academic journal priced at £5.95. No. 80, autumn 2000.
> **E1a.2** - Appeared in "Consuming for Pleasure" - United Kingdom: John Moore Press 2001 - paperback, ISBN: 0952797804. Edited by Julia Hallam and Nickianne Moody. Retitled as "The (dis)pleasures of Consuming: Extrapolations of Consumer Society in the Science Fiction of Michael Marshall Smith"

E2 MICHAEL MARSHALL SMITH: A PRIMARY AND SECONDARY BIBLIOGRAPHY

E2a - "Michael Marshall Smith: A Primary and Secondary Bibliography" - United Kingdom: Last Call Publishing 2000. Edited by Lavie Tidhar. 40 staple-bound copies in blue card wraps, priced at £5.00, no ISBN. Signed by LT, MMS, Stephen Jones, Jim Rickards and Archie Maskill. One set of A4 printer proofs were also produced.